A Study of Entrepreneurship Development among SC People in Indian Perspective

Dr. T. A. Kamble
Dr. S.S. Mahajan

KALPAZ

First Published, 2019

Published by

Kalpaz Publications
C-30, Satyawati Nagar,
Delhi – 110052
Ph.: 011-47034999, 9811692060
www.kalpazpublications.com
E-mail: kalpaz@hotmail.com

Printed at: G. Print Process, Delhi

Cataloging in Publication Data—DK

Courtesy: D.K. Agencies (P) Ltd. <docinfo@dkagencies.com>

Kamble, T. A., author.

A study of entrepreneurship development among SC people in Indian perspective / Dr. T.A. Kamble, Dr. S.S. Mahajan.

pages cm

Includes bibliographical references.

ISBN 9789353240004

1. Entrepreneurship—India. 2. Dalits—India—Economic conditions. I. Mahajan, S. S., author. II. Title.

LCC HB615.K36 2018 | DDC 338.040954 23

Contents

Preface

Entrepreneurship development has great significance in a country like India where occupations of people are based up on caste based stratification. Even today, directly or indirectly large portion of population is prevented from performing nontraditional, profit making and innovative economic activities for their livelihood. Socio economic development of people in marginalized and downtrodden community is lagging behind due to their traditionally forced engagement in unhygienic low paying and menial jobs. In recent past, especially after the independence, situation has been changing slowly. Constitutional protection and safe guards, Government efforts with defined reformative plans and policies, positive help from Non Government Agencies and institutions, have shown some positive results in the process of socio-economic development of these suppressed people. Apart from psychological sympathy and economic help, entrepreneurial opportunities are being provided to initiate new and innovative activities. Awareness of social, economic and entrepreneurial progress and its importance for them as well as for nation as whole are being inculcated among them. Many educated and aspiring youth from downtrodden community like Mahar, Mang, Chambhar, Dhor etc. are coming forward and trapping the entrepreneurial opportunities in business world. This is good and positive sign of transforming of society. Entrepreneurial opportunities for Dalit youth will certainly help not only for shaping their economic destiny and improving their social status but also it will help to create wealth and employment opportunities for our country.

Entrepreneurship development, especially in SC category is not merely depending upon social and economic support. Apart from this, purposeful attempt is required for inculcating and enhancing entrepreneurial skills, traits and competencies in them. Result oriented Entrepreneurship Development Programs (EDPs) with planned syllabi are to be conducted very seriously, that too, under the guidance and supervision of experts in this field, so that mindset and attitude of first generation entrepreneurs in SC category would be changed positively along with the improvement in their existing skills, traits and competencies.

In this writing, efforts are made to help aspiring entrepreneurs, especially from non business community in making them aware about entrepreneurship development and significance of it for their individual life as well as for society as whole. First chapter of this book deals with History of Entrepreneurship Development among SC People in Indian Perspective. Socio religious and occupational backdrop of these people is projected from the Vedic period to the present period of globalization.

In second chapter of this book, attempts are made to focus on Entrepreneurship Development and Significance of Business Environment. Many countrywide observations and findings from many research works with regards to environmental issues like religious castes, sub castes, family background, social movements, society and political support, education, changing State Policies etc. and their effect on entrepreneurship development process have been cited for exhibiting ground reality.

Third chapter of these books is devoted for Entrepreneurship Development Programs (EDPs), in which Significance of EDP, Objectives of EDP, Areas of EDP and Stages in EDP have been elaborated briefly. Apart from this, characteristics and qualities of successful entrepreneurs, essential skills, traits and competencies of successful entrepreneurs and functions of successful entrepreneurs have been discussed thoroughly.

Forth chapter of this book deals with Measurement of Entrepreneurship Development. In this chapter significance of measuring entrepreneurship development and its major indicators as well as attributes are highlighted at the beginning and attempts are made to assess Entrepreneurs hip Development Index (EDI). The formula of EDI is based up on formula of Human Development Index (HDI) developed by our great Indian economist and Nobel prize winner, Dr. Amrtya Sen and Dr. Sudhir Anand. Determination of major indicators and attributes therein was really challenging and thought provoking process. List of major indicators and its attributes is inclusive and not exhaustive. It is possible for any single entrepreneur or group of entrepreneurs in certain category to assess their entrepreneurship development with the help of defined formula and indicators contained therein.

Fifth and final chapter is devoted for SWOC Analysis of SC Entrepreneurs. In this chapter strengths weaknesses, possible opportunities and future challenges before SC entrepreneurs have been discussed. It is expected that, SC entrepreneurs are required to provide their attention seriously on these aspects.

This book is designed with view to stimulate the mind of young and energetic youth by taking reasonable risk and venture in to their own economics activities, rather than seeking the employment opportunities. This book will help to the students, researchers and faculty members of commerce and management. This book also will help to policy makers while framing their policies for the betterment of aspiring youths in downtrodden community through entrepreneurship development.

In the course of writing of this book we have referred many published and unpublished research articles, reference books, research projects, research theses and dissertations, reports of Government and Non Government Agencies. We acknowledge indebtedness of all the authors and publishers for their invaluable and path finding writing.

We would be happy and feel truly rewarded if this book satisfies our readers. Further we shall be grateful to them, if they provide us their valuable feedback to improve next edition of this book.

Happy Reading

Dr T. A. Kamble

Dr S. S. Mahajan

Acknowledgment

We acknowledge indebtedness of Hon'ble V. C. of Shivaji University Kolhapur, senior faculty members in Department of Commerce and Management Shivaji University Kolhapur as well as the faculty members in senior colleges affiliated to Shivaji University Kolhapur for extending their guidance and support in making this book more useful. We are immensely thankful to our Kalpaz Publication publishing this book with their gracious efforts. We express our sincere gratitude to our all respondents for their invaluable support in providing necessary information and data of their business and their existing skills, traits and competencies. We are thankful to Mr. Sarfraz Mulla, Director of Golden Computers, Chandgad for his painstaking efforts in typing and printing this book. Finally we are grateful to all those persons who have helped us directly or indirectly for making this book more meaningful.

Chapter - I

History of Entrepreneurship Development in SC People

1.1 Introduction

Entrepreneurship is a process of purposeful activities undertaken with reasonable risk, where the ideas are transformed into economic opportunities through the innovations. These economic opportunities shape the economic destiny of nation by creating wealth and employment, offering products and services and generating taxes for government. Being the major source of competitiveness, most of the governments at global level strive to augment supply of competent and globally competitive entrepreneurs in their respective countries. Most of the developed nations have reasonably good pace of entrepreneurial supply, while developing countries suffer from dearth of such entrepreneurs. This is one of the reasons for the poverty in developing countries despite their rich resource endowments.

Entrepreneurship has some elements of innovation and growth potential. Innovations bring higher productivity and enhance more competitiveness among the entrepreneurs. The role of entrepreneurs is not confined only to creation of enterprises, but also includes creation of the capacity to produce wealth, jobs, and income, which are most direct indicators of economic development. Moreover under development is not because of the lack of natural resources but because of the absence or inadequate supply of entrepreneurs. As a matter of fact, economic growth is the outcome of entrepreneurial endevours, as they pool together and organize various factors of production. They explore opportunities, convert ideas into viable business propositions leading to provision of new product and services to society. It changes the way of life.

The socio-economic development process of any country largely depend upon the proper functioning of business enterprises of that country, which inter alia depend upon entrepreneurship development. Entrepreneurship is one of the important aspects and means for the development of any economy. The role of entrepreneurs in socio-economic development varies from economy to economy and country to country. Entrepreneurship development is widely depending upon material resources, industrial climate and more importantly socio-economic, political responsiveness as well as educational and religious atmosphere in that country. It is because only the conducive and healthy atmosphere provide equal opportunities, significant support and encouragement to the entrepreneurs for their individual and common growth as well development of that society.

1.2 Entrepreneurship Development in Indian perspective

There are thousands of castes and sub-castes in India. In under developed country like India, caste and sub castes determines a social status of every person; Castes also determines the occupation of that particular person moreover castes decides the opportunities and scope of jurisdiction of their occupation. Taking into consideration the importance of caste factor, one cannot ignore the role of caste in entrepreneurship development. It matters much to assess the impact of castes and sub-castes of the people on entrepreneurial development in industrial sector.

According to John Kunkel[1], religion is an important component in all social factors, which influences very much on entrepreneurship development. He further observed that, social structure in which entrepreneurs were living and are being lived, affects either positively or negatively the behaviour of those entrepreneurs. In addition, their behaviour is also affected by social and economic motives. According to him, social structure, demand structure and opportunity structure limits the scope of entrepreneurial business. Being caste is the centre point of any social system especially in fundamentalist and orthodox country like India, at one side, people those are born in particular high class and reputed family, they avail all the opportunities provided under various entrepreneurial development schemes and on the other hand people those are born in socially and economically exploited, lower and ex-untouchable families are denied those opportunities despite their ability, creativeness and innovativeness.

While explaining the significant features of caste system in Indian perspective, Dr Ghurye[2], focused on influencing factors causing occupational mobility. According to him in caste based stratification, people have been classified on the principles of their occupations they do. It is because, the social status of an individual is determined according to the upper or lower class of their occupations. Each caste and sub-caste have their own traditional occupations. It is expected that people in each caste and sub-caste should perform their traditional occupations only. People cannot afford to choose own occupations according to their wish and liking. According to Dr Ghurye, as the occupations are based on caste based stratification, freedom to choose any other fair and profit-making occupation, other than their traditional one is denied. Every occupation is regulated and controlled by caste and religion and also it determines indirectly the economic condition of every person. In fact, In Indian social system, caste based occupational classification and distribution is one of the major reasons for economic backwardness of Scheduled Castes (ex – untouchable) entrepreneurs.

In India, category of Scheduled Castes people is a major segment of Hindu religion.They were suppressed socially and exploited economically from thousands of years, from Hindu upper caste people. In past they were neither treated as human being nor they allowed to awaken from their slavery.Further neither they permitted to take education nor were they guided towards their social and economic upliftment. Now, however situation and atmosphere is being changed. Especially since the independence, many people from Scheduled Caste category are emerged as well known entrepreneurs, from all the aspects of vocation and profession, throughout India, due to invaluable efforts taken by great social reformers like Jyotirao Phule, Chh. Shahu Raje, Dr Babasaheb Ambedkar etc. in pre-independence period. Now attempts are being made by the State and Central Government to remove social and economical barriers through their policies and strategies. Opportunities are being provided to them, for their personal as well as occupational development. Awareness of social, economic and entrepreneurial progress and the changes are being inculcated among downtrodden people. The Constitution of India prescribes protection and safeguards for Scheduled Castes with an object of removing their social disabilities and protecting their varied interest. The main safeguards are – abolition of untouchability, protection from social injustice and various forms of exploitations, opening all the religious places and temples to all the out castes, removal of restrictions on access to shops, restaurants, wells, tanks and roads, giving them right to move freely and acquire property, admission to all educational institutions, receiving grants from the State, reservations in educational institutions, government and semi-Government service sectors, reservations in Local Bodies, State Assembly and Parliament, establishment of financial institutions, training centres etc. Government has passed various Acts and Laws to abolish the castesm and ill practices in social system and protection is provided to the SC people in the country. It is a good and positive sign of socio-economic change in India. Apart from many hardships, lack of resources and prevalent caste prejudice, entrepreneurs in SC category feel proud of being an entrepreneurs. Now some of them are in position to assist others in establishing their enterprises or providing them employment. But this is not enough. Despite, several positive changes, there are several factors like caste system, economic backwardness, lack of sufficient opportunities in education and further entry in industrial, finance, marketing and service sector, those are playing negative role. Now it is the high time to assess critically the growth and entrepreneurial development among SC people, and guide this movement towards proper destination.

Majority of SC people in India as well as in Maharashtra are engaged in their traditional, unhygienic, low skilled and lower income vocation, especially leather tanning, shoe making, roads and toilet cleaning, making ropes of whemps, bamboo articles,gavaki and veth bigar and allied work of cleaning etc. Such mean work is done by them despite having ambitions, skills and abilities in them needed for any business. The customs and traditional norms do not allow them to become entrepreneurs. If they attempt any such new and innovative business, society do not permit them to do so. In order to boost their confidence, to raise their standard of living, to upgrade their social and economic status, it is necessary to divert them towards some other innovative business opportunities. They should encourage for obtaining vocational and professional training required for their innovative businesses.

Today India is the young country with majority of population being in the working age group of 15 to 59 years, but unless we engage our youth in creative pursuits through developing their appropriate skills, including entrepreneurship skill, positive result will not reflect in the development of our economy. In India, what we find is, our society, our culture, our educational system rarely exposes our youth for entrepreneurship. Even if someone with high entrepreneurial aspiration wants to setup a business, he or she is discouraged by a host of adverse factors. Lack of adequate access to information, lack of seed capital as well as lack of technological, managerial and mentoring support hinder the emergence of entrepreneurship. On this background, our policy makers and society at large should make an honest attempt to create healthy and supportive environment for the emergence of more and more entrepreneurs. Focus should be given on motivating the aspired persons, providing business opportunities and developing essential skills in them. This will encourage the people to venture out. Government and society should help them in creating an entrepreneurial awareness and developing their skills. Government should try to change the mindset of target group. Serious attempts should be made to initiate entrepreneurship movement, especially in non-business downtrodden communities.

1.3 History of Scheduled Caste People (Ex-Untouchables) In India

According to Dr B. R. Ambedkar[3], the practice of untouchability began from Vedic times. Although, in those days Shudras were treated as socially equal to the Brahmin, Kshatriya, and Vaish Varnas, their participation in religious rituals was considered to be defiling. In Vedic literature we come across many injunctions and hurdles affecting persons to perform *Yadnya.* Neither untouchables were allowed to participate in pooja path nor were they allowed talking with others at the time of performing pooja. If at all any communication had been taken place, savarn people were used to take holy bath before performing pooja and before taking meal. These untouchables were separated from rest of the society due to the customs of ugly untouchability. Untouchables remain untouchable from birth to death.

Dr B. R. Ambedkar observed that, every caste is attributed with certain degree of ritual purity right at the time of birth and for preserving this level; every caste has to observe rules and rituals prescribed by the religion. However untouchables do not possess any degree of purity, and hence they are treated untouchables forever, even if they behave well and pursue clean occupation due to dirty traditional beliefs.

The Structure of Hindu social system; as observed by Dr Babasaheb Ambedkar is as under-

Hindu
↓
Savarna Hindu | Avarna Hindu

Savarna Hindu ↓

Class I
(High Castes)
1. Brahmin
2. Kshatriya
3. Vaishya

Class II
(Low Castes)
Shudras
(Separated from
Kshatriya)

Avarna Hindu ↓

Class III
1. Prime Tribes
2. Criminal Tribes

Class IV
Untouchables
(SC people)

Fig. 1.1 Structure of Hindu Social System

According to Govind Sharma[4] the Hindu social system and its classification made by *Manu Rishi*, the architect of *Manusmriti*, held that, Hindu social order is repulsive in nature (i.e. strong feeling of dislike) right from class II to class IV, The untouchables being the representative of class IV are the most disgusting people in the Hindu social system. These untouchables were known as *Chandal, Patita, Achut, Shudras, out caste* and so on. They ware called depressed classes, in Census Reports and in common political parlance till 1925. In 1931 Census this terms was replaced yet another connotation, the "Exterior Castes", while in 1936 these peoples were started calling Scheduled Castes after issuing Scheduled Castes Order 1936, which was based upon Government of India Act. 1935.

1.4. National and State Level Distribution of SC Population

The statistics of SC population[5] at national and state level for the last three decades is shown in the following table.

1.5 Socio-Religious and Occupational Backdrop of SC People in Maharashtra

1.5.1 Vedic Period: Apart from social and religious hardship on untouchables, Rishi Manu, in his *Manusmriti*[5] says, god, the creator of earth, has given birth to shudra only to serve Brahmin and all other upper caste people, even if his owner (Brahmin) escaped from his inherited slavery. It is for the simple reason that, by birth, slavery is the ultimate colleague of them. Manu, further declared that Shudras and untouchables are not permitted to collect and save the funds as well as property for their well being, even if they are able and worthy to do so, as it causes harm and create pains to the Brahmin people.

Table No 1.1: Distribution of Census wise SC Population

Sr. No	*Area of Population*	*Census 1991*	*Census 2001*	*Census 2011*
	India			
1.	Total population of India	64,13,02,688	1,02,64,43,540	1,21,01,93,422
2.	Total SC population of India	13,82,23,277	16,65,75,663	16,66,35,700
3.	% of SC population to total population of India	21.56%	16.23%	13.76%
	Maharashtra state			
1.	Total population of Maharashtra	7,89,37,187	9,68,78,627	11,23,74,333
2.	Total SC population of Maharashtra	87,57,842	98,81,656	1,32,75,898
3.	% of SC population to total population of Maharashtra	11.09%	10.20%	11.80%

Source: Census of India 1991, 2001, and 2011.

1.5.2 Spiritual Saint Period: During the period of 12th century, the high class spiritual saint, divine thinkers and social reformers like Dnyaneshwar, Ramadas, Ekanath, Tukaram etc. surrendered themselves before inelastic and inhuman caste system in Hindu religion, and they too supported caste based discrimination through their so-called holy and popular literature.

Saint Dyaneshwar[6] said about low caste shudras and untouchables that they have no other alternate religion, but to serve the Brahmin and all other upper caste people. Dyaneshwar[7] further admitted that shudras and other lower caste people have no religious right to perform Vedic rites, As one cannot avoid the colour of his body, shudra and other lower caste people shall never avoid their dirty and unhygienic occupations those are explained in Varnas. Spiritual Saint Dnyaneshwar[8]further pleaded that, Brahmins are the god of this earth, and all the holy, religious places are emerged due to their Vedic rituals and worships.

Saint Eknath[9], in his Eknathi Bhagwat explained ten each eternal qualities or the features of Brahmins and Kshatriyas, five qualities of Vaihyas, two qualities of Shudras and four qualities of Atishrdras (untouchables). According to Eknath, Brahmin always should be busy in Vedic and spiritual activities. He should never afraid of cold, wind, rain and hot summer. He always remain calm and quite in all circumstances. He must show his kindness, love and affection to all poor and depressed peoples. He should never thinks over untrue and unfair facts. He should always seems happy and fully satisfied.

According to Ekanath, Kshatriyas are powerful and courageous emperor. They are mighty. Their duties are to protect cows and Brahmins and their praja (people in kingdom). They are the extreme donors, never hesitate to donate their all kinds of wealth available with them, to the Brahmins and the beggars, coming to them. Kshatriya can achieve their name, fame and wealth only when they pray Brahmins with sincere and happy state of mind.

Ekanath further elaborated the eternal features of Vaishyas. Vaishyas are born for doing trade and commercial activities. They are very greedy for wealth and money. They keep deep faith on Vedas and Shastras. They are supposed to donate their wealth and money to the Brahmins and baggers until their death. They are expected to offer their services to the Brahmins and make them happy.

According to Ekanath,Shudras are born only for offering their services to the Brahmins and upper caste people and to take care of cows and other animals of them. Atishudras or the untouchables are dirty and worst person, who are supposed to live outside of the village, they are the cheaters, thieves and dacoities. Shudras and Atishudras i.e. untouchables are not worthy to learn or listen Ved-Shastras and other religious literature.

Samarth Ramdas[10],in his Dasbodh proudly says that caste based and religious discrimination is the creation of god, and all the Hindu people are supposed to live in accordance with those discriminations. All the discriminations in Hindu social system are done by the god. Even if the low caste person or untouchables, is worthy and possess the qualities of good teacher, or the guide, he cannot afford to teach or guide to others as basically it is the duty of Brahmin. The Brahmin only has right of possess these qualities. If any untouchables are doing so, it will be treated as the violation of rules laid down by the god.

1.5.3.Mediaeval Muslim Regime: In Mediaeval Muslim Regime[11] the lower orders (untouchables) of the society were badly treated and were subject of humiliation. It was the practice of engaging untouchables and Dalits, landless peoples as bonded labours, by the Muslim rulers especially for constructing forts, huge dams, roads and mosques. They were also used for excavation of mines, khandakas around the forts and palaces etc. Many untouchables and Dalits engaged in such hard work had to runaway leaving behind their wives and children due to humiliating and inhuman treatment they received.

In Muslim regime, castes were not allowed to change their occupations. Untouchables like Mahar, Mang, Chambhar etc. had to follow their traditional and unhygienic occupations those were based on Hindu religious system. At that time, it was treated that, performing the traditional and caste based occupations is an order of god and everybody has to follow it.

1.5.4 Peshwa Period: Under the Peshwa regime[12], in every sphere of social, religious, economic and cultural life, principles and thoughts explained in Manusmriti were acting as deciding factors. Social systems based on castes and classes had become rigid one. Shudras and untouchables were not treated even as human being too.

In Poona town, untouchable peoples like Mahar, Mang etc. were not allowed to walk on the road from the sunrise till 9 o'clock in the morning, and from 4 o'clock till sunset in the evening, so as to avoid the shadow of those people. It was inferred that, if the shadow is fallen on the Brahmin, It becomes the matter of vital i.e. impure. Untouchables had to tie a muddy pot in their neck and broom around their waist. Muddy pot was for spinting purpose and broom was for wipe off their foot prints.

So far as occupation[13] are concerned, Shudras and untouchables were required to follow strictly their traditional unhygienic dirty occupations, as stated in ManuSmriti and Dharmashastras. People who attempted to do other jobs or occupations were punished severely. The untouchables those were engaged in serving upper caste people; either they had to accept Vethbigari. (i.e Service without pay) or had to divert towards criminal activities for their livelihood.

1.5.5 Pre Independence Period

1.5.5.1 Jyotirao Phule: Jyotirao Phule[14], the great social reformer in Maharashtra fought against slavery, inhumanism and traditional untouchability observed by Hindu upper caste people, (i.e. Brahmin people) behind the shelter of so-called holy Vedas and religious books like Manusmriti, Vedshastras etc. In the Pune city of Peshwas, where traditional customs vedic rites and rituals were observed very rigidly and the walls of castes and sub-castes had been created among human being, since the ages. Jyotirao Phule kicked off the traditional culture and custom derived from Vedas and Purans, those were denying humanism since thousands of years. He wanted to destruct those caste based walls. He opened up his own water tank to the thirsty untouchables in Pune. He started school for Mahar people in the heart of the Pune city to educate them and encouraged his wife 'Savitribai' to work as teacher in that school.

Jyotirao Phule, who always coupled his thoughts with his act, certainly knew that, unless and until untouchables are not educated, they will not awake, from their slavery and think over their development. While educating the people in lower classes as well as women in society and inculcating the thoughts of social equality in them, Jyotirao and his wife Savitribai had to face many problems. Especially, Brahmin people in Pune city humiliated them worstly.

Despite all those facts, Jyotirao and his wife encouraged untouchables to take education and upgrade them socially and economically. Further, Jyotirao Phule witnessed before Hunter commission in 1853 and exhibited new theory of education which goes from classes to masses. He strongly opposed to the theory of filtration which was preventing the educational right of common people and strongly insisted for bottom to top educational system, where lower order people could develop themselves in real sense.

1.5.5.2 Chh. Shahu Raje:[15] The king of Kolhapur Sansthan (State) and the greatest social reformer in Maharashtra, Chh. Shahu Raje had tried to provide social equality in his state. He wanted to destruct man-made social barriers created by Brahmin people with the help of Vedas and Shastras and also wanted to provide an equal opportunity to suppressed people from thousands of years in his state.

Chh. Shahu started night schools in Kolhapur Sansthan for untouchables like Mahar, Mang, Chambhar etc. to educate them and their children. Initially, he established separate school for female children and women, especially for Chambhar and Dhor community and later on established common school to all people so as to eradicate the caste based discrimination existed in since the ages. Chh. Shahu Raje also sponsored and made available free and compulsory education to all. And spent lakhs of rupees for that purpose.

Chh. Shahu had given an opportunity to the elementary educated untouchables like Mahar, Mang, Chambhar, Dhor etc. to work as *Daptarbandh* in Revenue Department of his state and also given an opportunities of promotions to those, who shown skill, intelligence and progress in their work. Chh. Shahu Raje passed an ordinance, prohibiting untouchability in public places, declaring punishable with imprisonment along with fine, to the village officer, (Talathi) and Chief of village, (Gao Kamgar Patil) where untouchability ordinance is violated by them. He eliminated *Balutedari* and *Vethbigari* system of work, throughout the territory of his state and encouraged lower caste people including untouchables to give up their unhygienic and dirty occupation forced on them by Hindu caste system. He allotted licenses and provided required finance to the needy untouchables to choose and conduct new, innovative and liking occupations instead of old and unhygienic traditional occupation. He helped untouchables like Gangaram Kamble to establish small hotel in Kolhapur city where he always used to go for having tea.

1.5.5.3. Dr Babasaheb Ambedkar: Dr B. R. Ambedkar[16] the greatest nation builder and social reformer believes that Brahmnik theory of origin of Shudras, status were one of the *Aryan Community*, of the solar race. It was the time when Aryan Society recognised only three 'varnas' namely Brahmin, Kshatriya and Vaishya. The shudras did not form a separate varna, in fact Shudras were originally belongs to 'Kshatriyas' separated and socially degraded by the Brahmins due to feud between them.

According to Dr B. R. Ambedkar, caste based gradation and unequal Hindu social system creates varieties of deprivations to untouchables, in India as well as in Maharashtra. Untouchability was not just religious matter, but a stigma imposed on the untouchables, which deprives them of the basic economic and social rights, free access to the civil amenities such as wells, schools, village temples. They could not avail the services of Barber, Washerman etc. They did not allow to wear gold and silver ornaments and also they did not permitted to dress like higher caste people. It is evident that, the practice of untouchability had produced many harmful consequences in the social, economic and political sphere of their life. The religious notion of purity and impurity in Hindu society created untouchable castes and were made to follow unclean occupation.

According to Dr Ambedkar, the occupations those were performed traditionally are considered to be ritually impure and connected with dirt and unhygienic. According to him 'Savarna' people can maintain their ritual purity only if the untouchables perform their so-called occupations.

Dr Babasaheb Ambedkar[17] awakened to the untouchables in India from their everlasting sleep of slavery. He made them aware about their socio-religious degraded status, in Hindu caste system and asked them to giveup their traditional and inhuman occupations, preventing them from worshipping the Hindu Gods and obeying Vedas and Dharma shastras. He enlightened the light of self respect in them, advised to take education, appealed them to come together and fight for their socio-economic rights.

Dr Babasaheb Ambedkar being the creator of Indian Constitution, made many constitutional provisions for the well-being and development of suppressed untouchables in India. These provisions really helped them in availing social, political, educational and economic equality for their betterment. Equal opportunities are being provided for their overall development, only because of strong constitutional provisions.

1.5.6 Post Independence Period: Nationwide Socio-Religious and Occupational Situation: According to John Kunkel, India being tradition and custom oriented country, where religion is accounted as an important factor in all social factors, influences very much especially on an entrepreneurship. The social structure, demand structure and opportunity structure limits the scope of the entrepreneurial business. Being caste is the centre point of any social system, especially in fundamentalist orthodox Hindu religion at one side, the people those are born in particular high class family, having strong socio-economic support are availing all the entrepreneurial opportunities provided under various development schemes in post independence period, and on the other hand people those are belongs to lower strata (i.e. ex-untouchables) they are denied those opportunities despite their creativeness and innovativeness. A Socio-economic barrier imposes the limit on their creativity.

As observed by E.W. Nafziger[18], entrepreneurs born in higher castes are economically prosperous and educationally sound. They have enough experiences in entrepreneurial activities. They easily avail sufficient capital, government aid and assistance in various schemes. As their social status and economical position is safe and sound, consequently, they progress speedily in their entrepreneurial activities. Researcher M. U. Deshpande[19] supported this fact and admitted that, majority of entrepreneurs in Maharashtra region are belonging to higher class of society and of course they are socially and economically forward. The caste is the major factor among all other socio-economic and educational factors which has influenced considerably over the entrepreneurship. He further admitted that all the aid and assistance provided by the Government was grabbed by those high class society entrepreneurs.

According to Surinder S. Jodhaka[20], caste variables almost and always playing a negative role for Dalits (ex-untouchables) entrepreneurs, especially while raising the finance and acquiring the business locations. As per his observation in UP and Haryana, SC entrepreneurs are experiencing caste related discrimination in their personal and day-to-day life. Caste affects their business negatively. The social universe of the business has been so completely controlled by certain caste communities that, at the time when SC entrepreneurs come into business, they being hate and call upon with caste name. According to him, SC entrepreneurs are facing hardship due to lack of resources and caste prejudice. Despite several positive changes, caste continues to play a vital role (almost negative) in their progress.

Surinder S. Jodhka further observed that SC entrepreneurs started to consolidate themselves after 1980. Few of them diverted themselves in to new and non-traditional occupations. Virtually most of them are first generation entrepreneurs.Education and economic motivational factors have been playing positive role in changing their attitude towards occupations. Their major sources of motivations are better dignity, self respect, better standards of living and also doing something meaningful, which would not only give them income and dignity but also generate employment for others.

Despite all the social and economic barriers, SC entrepreneurs are finding their space and positions in entrepreneurial world. Due to success in business they found much easier to enter into mainstream of political space, and this help SC entrepreneurs as a shield, in their business and individual sphere of life.

According to Z Mars[21] in Kerela, traditional occupation of any family, the means of production, available to them and the area of entrepreneurship selected by the family members are correlated with each others and it determines and assists in achieving entrepreneurial success. Entrepreneurs especially in Maharashtra are found from comparatively well known Zamindar and upper caste families having political hold and thereby they avail economic and non-economic Government aid and assistance for their entrepreneurial betterment. This helps them in achieving professional education, skill, competitiveness and thereby occupational success.

Mr Gangrade K. D.[22], While doing his research study on "Social Mobility in India, a study of depressed class," in Chattera village in state of Haryana, observed that most of the respondents are disassociated themselves from their traditional occupations with strong desire to improve and attain their higher status.

D. Narendra kumar[23] observed in Chittur district of Andhra State, entrepreneurs belongs to socially and religiously upper castes, categories, holds monopoly over entire small scale industrial sector and most of the political and economic support was limited to them only.

R. Madhavan[24], talking about Chettiar Community in southern part of India, is one of major community with rich entrepreneurial heritage. The credit of success goes to their inherited professional business approach and their entrepreneurial family background.

1.6 Conclusion

Previously SC people in India were not allowed to perform fair, hygienic and high rewarding occupations, as they were suppressed socially and exploited economically from the hands of upper caste people in Hindu religion. Caste based stratified social system was preventing them from having equal opportunities in every sphere of their life. Now these SC people are performing traditional as well as high rewarding and choice based occupations.

According to Davis and Blomstorm[25], our modern view of society is an ecological one. Ecology is concern with mutual relation with human population or the system with their environment. It is necessary to take broad view, because the influence and involvement of business are extensive. Business cannot isolate itself from rest of the society. Today, the whole society is charged with the business environment. In short business is an integral part of today's social system. It is a social organ to help and accomplish the social goal. On this background co-operation, assistance and encouragement being received by the society at large to SC entrepreneurs is disappointing one.In the order to bring SC people in the main stream of national development, it is indeed necessary to support them economically; morally, in addition, it is necessary to make them aware of their potent skills and capacities. Moreover some confidence building measures are needed for overall development of these people.

References

1. John Kunkel, (1970), Society and Economic Growth: A Behavioural Perspective of Social Changes, Oxford University Press London, pp. 260-270, quoted by Dr Prabhakar Deshmukh, Udyojakta Vikas Pipalapure Prakashan Nagpur, 2002.
2. G.S. Ghurye, (1978), Caste, Class and Occupation, Popular Book Depot. Mumbai. p. 142, quoted by V. N. Gajendragadkar, Castes, Races in India.
3. Dr B.R. Ambedkar's (1989), Writing and Speeches Vol. 5, Vol. 7, Government of Maharashtra.
4. Govind Sharma, (1984), Trends in the Study of Scheduled Castes, The Journal of Indian Anthropological Association New Delhi, Vol. 14, p. 119.
5. Census of India, (2011), Government of India.
6. Shankarrao Kharat, (2006), Samajik Chalvalicha Itihas, Indrayani Prakashan, Pune. p. 151.
7. *Ibid* p. 887.
8. *Ibid* p. 476.
9. Shankarrao Kharat, (2006), Samajik Chalvalicha Itihas, Indrayani Prakashan, Pune, retrieved from Saint Eknath, Eknathi Bhagwat, Shlok 17 to 19, pp. 697 to 701. Adhyay 17-82, 17-83, pp. 693 to 702.

10. Shankarrao Kharat, (2006) Samajik Chalvalicha Itihas, Indrayani Prakashan, Pune,Retrieved from Samarth Ramdas, Dasbodh 13, samas 10, Ovi 13, p. 523, Dasbodh 14, Samas 14, Ovi 29, p. 553, Dasbodh 17, Samas 10, Ovi 20, p. 658.
11. Shankarrao Kharat, (2006), Samajik Chalvalicha Itihas, Indrayani Prakashan, Pune, Retrieved from Prof M.S. Mate, Problems of Untouchables p. 143.
12. N.V.Joshi (Ed), (2001), Ravindra Thakur, Pune Varnan, Mudra Prakashan, Kolhapur, p. 61.
13. Shankarrao Kharat, (2006), Samajik Chalvalicha Itihas, Indrayani Prakashan, Pune. p. 151.
14. *Ibid.,* pp. 221 to 231.
15. P.B.Salunkhe, M.G.Mali(Ed.), (1994), Chh. Shahu, the Pillar of Social Democracy, Education Dept. Government of Maharashtra, pp. 28 to 45.
16. Dr B.R. Ambedkar, (1989), Rock on which Hindu have built Their Houses, Dr Babasaheb Ambedkar's writing and speeches Vol. 5 Government of Maharashtra.
17. Shankarrao Kharat (Ed.) (2006), Dr Babsaheb Ambedkar Yanchi Atmakatha, Indrayani Sahitya Prakashan,pp 40-41.
18. E.W. Nafzigar, (Jan 1975), Class, Caste and Community of South India Industrialist; An Examination of Horatio Alger Model In The Journal Of Development Studies Vol. II, No. 2, pp. 131 To 148.
19. M.U. Deshpande, (1964), Entrepreneurship of Small Scale Industries, Deep and Deep Publication, New Delhi, p. 282.
20. Surindar S. Jodhaka, (Nov. 2010), Dalits in Business; Self Employed Scheduled Castes in Northwest India, Working Paper Series Vol. IV, By Indian Institute of Dalit Studies.
21. Z. Mars, (1975), Assistance to Small Scale Industries In Kerala, An Indian Case, In Development of Changes Vol. XVI No. 2, pp. 14 to 18.
22. K.D. Gangrde,(1975), Social Mobility in India, a Study of Depressed Class, Man in India, Vol. No. 53, Sept. p. 252,
23. D. Narendra Kumar (1995), Entrepreneurship in Small Scale Sector, Discovery Publishing House, New Delhi, pp. 150 To 161.
24. R. Madhavan, (Jan 28 Feb 4), Pattern of Enterprises of Chattiare, In Malaya, 1880 To 1930, Economic and Political Weekly Vol. 13 No. 4-5, pp. 146 To 154.
25. Kith Devis and Blomstrom, (1971), Business Society and Environment, McGraw Hill, New York, p. 11.

Chapter - II

Entrepreneurship Development and Significance of Business Environment

2.1. Introduction

A study of socio-economic, political, educational and all other domestic nature of environment is an important aspect of entrepreneurship development for any entrepreneur in any country. The speed, level and quality of its development is largely depend upon such environmental issues existed in that particular country. All the business plans and strategies of an entrepreneur are mostly based on it. These environmental issues regulates all the business activities conducted by any entrepreneur. Therefore, these issues must be taken into consideration all the time, while planning, organizing and co-ordinating business activities.

2.2. Types of Business Environment and its Significance

2.2.1. Political Environment: Political environment deals with Government plans and policies, generally which determines industrial and licensing policies, foreign exchange regulations, banking and investment policies, formation and implications of various commercial Acts and Laws, imposing taxes and duties, reservation policies etc. Promotion of entrepreneurship and its development is mostly dependingup on political responsiveness. If the political environment is supportive, it encourages a lot to initiate more business enterprises and also helps to foster entrepreneurship to a greater extent. On the other hand if the political environment is not supportive, it creates hurdles in it.

2.2.2. Economic Environment: Economic environment deals with financial status of an individual and his or her family, investment capacity, sources of funds, expenditure incurred on raising finance, banking and financial system, rules, regulations and policies of central banks with regards to finance and investment, rate of return on investment made etc. Entire entrepreneurial growth and development is depend upon such economic environmental issues. Further quality of raw material, cost of production, cost of sale and capacity to earn profit also are the considerable economic factors. Healthy market atmosphere especially in financial market boosts entrepreneurship development and vice versa.

2.2.3. Social and Cultural Environment: Social and cultural environment deals with religions, castes, sub-castes, traditions, rules and regulations governing various castes and sub-castes. Many social scientist believe that, entrepreneurial growth and development is significantly depend up on, even today, on social atmosphere available in particular region. In a country like India, where religion and castes are centre point of social system it greatly affects on occupational mobility and ultimately it affects on earning capacity of a person conducting his business. History reveals that, especially in Hindu social system, lower castes people are supposed to engage in low paying, unhygienic, dead end and menial work despite of their intelligence and competencies and upper castes people are motivated to conduct innovative, profit making and prestigious business activities. Thus entrepreneurship development is closely associated with society support and social atmosphere available for particular entrepreneur. If the social environment is supportive and healthy, overall entrepreneurship development fosters speedily and if social environment is unhealthy and non-supportive, it creates hurdles in it.

2.2.4. Educational and Technological Environment: Educational environment deals with types of and quality of education perceived by the people in a country, it also deals with inculcation of values, application of scientific knowledge, cultural and technological advancement, behavioural changes and improvement in quality of life of people. Educational and technological environment enhances not only the profit of entrepreneurs but also maintains balance in the eco-system for society. If the educational and technological environment is sound, healthy and supportive, comparatively good quality of entrepreneurs emerges with superior quality of products and vice versa.

2.2.5. Legal Environment: Legal environment includes enactment of various Acts, Laws, Code of Conduct etc. to regulate business world, especially with regards to registration of business organisations, providing licenses, prohibiting pollution, protection of environment, controlling and prohibiting malpractices, payment of wages and benefits after retirement, payment of taxes etc. Legal environment is closely associated with political environment. If the political environment is free, healthy and supportive, legal environment automatically remains healthy and supportive, which ultimately encourage for entrepreneurial development and if political environment is unhealthy and non-supportive legal environment get suffer adversely and badly affects on creation and development of entrepreneurial activities.

2.3 Major Observations and Finding with regards to Entrepreneurship Development

2.3.1 Religions, Castes, Sub-Castes and Entrepreneurship Development: Religions, castes, and sub-castes of entrepreneurs and their entrepreneurial development have close relation with each other. Following are the major findings in this regard.

1. H.A. Milman (1954)[1] found that, traditional and ongoing customs, domestic atmosphere, value system, motivation from family members etc. are the reasons, which keeps process of creating entrepreneurs continuously. Especially in Marwadi community, the values inculcated, formal as well as informal education and training imparted, economic and moral support provided to their young entrepreneurs fosters and enhance the skill, capabilities and competence of them. Children in Marwadi family get the regular guidance and every kind of support from their elders. They are participated directly in their own occupation and they are asked to hold responsibilities gradually. Their business activities are observed by the seniors and guidance is provided as and when necessary. As their potentialities are developed thoroughly, they are asked to handle the business independently. Thus, in Marawadi society, systematic and serious efforts are taken to develop young child in to matured entrepreneur.

2. Max Webber (1958)[2] has researched on comparative study of guiding principles of Hindu, Muslim, and Buddha religion, in Eastern countries. According to him, Hindu people believe in divine spirituality, rebirth rites and observance. Their attitude towards life is ascetic. The Hindu religion does not support the values and thoughts like entrepreneurs, achievement, money, property, economic development etc. Therefore the concept of entrepreneur and entrepreneurship development is not rooted in them to the required extent. As the Hindu religion is unconcern about risk bearing, facing uncertainties, achieving success, developing business etc, there is lack of motivation about economic development. Being SC people are the major segment of Hindu religion, all these attributes are associated with them also.

3. J. J. Barna (1960)[3] found that despite lower religious status of SC entrepreneurs, their strong wish of becoming successful entrepreneur, their education and training programmes, their consistent hard work and innovations, SC entrepreneurs made them possible to become successful entrepreneurs.

4. R. Madhavan (1963)[4] while studying about Chettiare community in Southern part of India, observed that, Chettiare is one of the major communities with rich entrepreneurial heritage. Despite having different kinds of business atmosphere, culture and hindrances, they secured their own standard in India as well as at abroad. The main credit of their success goes to their inherited professional business approach. Their domestic atmosphere and background always motivate them to create successful entrepreneurs. His research work infers that entrepreneurship development is lot more depend upon rich entrepreneurial heritage and domestic atmosphere as it motivate successfully to the entrepreneurs even belongs to SC category.

5. M. U. Deshpande (1964)[5] found that the entrepreneurs in Scheduled Caste, Scheduled Tribes and Other Backward Class are meager (negligible) in small scale industrial sector of Marathwada. Researcher found all the entrepreneurs in that sector, those were belongs to higher class of society. These entrepreneurs were socially and economically forward. The 'caste' was the major factor among all other social economic and religious factors, which influenced over their entrepreneurship.

6. Ito Shoji (1966)[6] has studied on entrepreneurship in Chettiare community. He found that this community in Southern India is advanced one in their entrepreneurial activities due to traditional and inherited professional approach and domestic entrepreneurial background.

7. Liberson S. (et.al) (1967)[7] observed that, Negroes in USA were brought as slaves and after abolition of slavery they employed in the manual and non-profitable jobs, for centuries until recently. It was informed that, racial dissimilarities in occupation structure declined with each succeeding generation, but at a rather slow rate. Researchers further observed that, Non Whites are still occupationally disadvantaged. Despite the equality in formal educational attainment, they did not obtain the same job as White.

It was further reported that, Negroes were over represented in lower jobs and less chances were left for employing as manager, proprietor, sales worker and a like.

8. Almendu Guha (1970)[8] has tried to identify the effect of caste-system on entrepreneurship. While explaining on success achieved by Parasi entrepreneurs in Zorashtrian religion, observed that, the philosophy of Zorashtrain religion itself motivates and ask its followers to accept occupational responsibilities. Apart from this, the factors like good command over English language, closeness to the British peoples in India, European systems of organizing business, discovering new markets, and the last but not least, an honest attempt to cope up with the changing situation are responsible factors for their success.

9. John Kunkel (1970)[9] observed that, the social structure in which entrepreneurship were living and are being lived, affects either positively or negatively the behaviour of those entrepreneurs. In addition, their behaviour is also affected by social and economic motives. According to Kunkel, the social structure, demand structure and opportunity structure limits the scope of entrepreneurial success. John Kunkel admitted that religion is an important component in all social factors, which influences very much on entrepreneurship.

10. B.S. Bhatia (1974)[10] found that, most of the entrepreneurs achieved their success mainly due to their entrepreneurial experience and capital adequacy made available to them. He further observed that, neither particular so-called upper caste had dominance over industrial progress nor caste factor held responsible for their success and progress.

11. E.W.Nafzigar (1975)[11] found that the efficiency, motivation and final success are certainly affected by caste factor. Nafzigar observed that, entrepreneurs born in higher castes are economically prosperous and educationally sound.

12. G. S. Ghurye (1978)[12] focused on influencing factors causing occupational mobility. He found that in caste based stratification, people have been classified on the principles of their occupations they do. It is because, the social status of an individual is determined according to the upper or lower class of their occupations. Each caste and sub-caste having its own traditional occupations. It is expected that people in each caste and subcaste should perform their traditional occupations only. People cannot afford to choose their own occupations according to their wish and liking. Dr Ghurye further observed that as the occupations are based on caste based stratification, freedom to choose any other fair and profit making occupation, other than their traditional one is denied. Every occupation is regulated and controlled by caste and religion and also it determines indirectly the economic condition of every person. In fact, in Indian social system, caste based occupational classification and distribution is one of the major reasons for economic backwardness of Scheduled Castes (ex – untouchable) entrepreneurs.

13. R. A. Sharma (1980)[13] found that entrepreneurship development and castes of entrepreneurs are closely associated with each other. Further he observed that, now-a-days some people in upper class society are engaged in trading, manufacturing, financing investment etc. activities and people from lower caste category also now initiating and conducting their new business activities successfully despite their non-entrepreneurial background. Though entrepreneurs from lower caste category are financially and technologically weak, though they are lacking financial and managerial support as well as advanced marketing system,their entrepreneurial urge and motivation of getting success is quite high as comparative to traditional high class category entrepreneurs.

14. S. M. Dahiwale (1989)[14] found that there is positive association between young age and modern jobs. The interesting observation of his research was that, especially Chambhar community people are less prone to adopt modern occupations than other castes persons.They are remained engaged in their leather activities, as they have enough scope even in these changing times. He further observed that the respondents who possessed modern education, professional or vocational skill, have found easier to do modern jobs and those who remained still deprived of education or have remained less educated are doing their traditional jobs, The finding of this study was evident that, ex-untouchable persons are coming forward so as to gain an advantage of the changing times and are entering into jobs of middle occupational categories of the modern professional market.

15. Dr B. R. Ambedkar (1989)[15] has strongly argues that, Hindu religion has made caste system, divine and scarred things. He also pointed out that the economic activity has always remained outside the sanctity of religion. Hunting society also was not without religion, but hunting as an occupation was not made sacred the religion. Hindus are only people in the world whose economic order relation of workman to workman is concentrated by religion and made sacred eternal and inviolate.

16. D. P. Pandit (1995)[16] found that, in Gujarati social system, the people who are entrepreneurs, have better status other than non-entrepreneurs. The people engaged in business of trading and industrial activities are receiving special recognition name and fame, from Gujarati people. This fact motivates other people in Gujarat to become an entrepreneur.

17. D. Narendrakumar (1995)[17] observed that entrepreneurs belongs to socially and religiously upper class category hold monopoly over entire small scale industrial sector in Chittur district, as the entrepreneurial and social support was limited to this upper class only.

18. Prabhakar Deshmukh (2002)[18] stated that, there are thousands of castes and sub-castes in India. In a underdeveloped country like India, castes and sub-castes determines a social status of every person. Castes also determine the occupation of particular persons. Moreover castes decides the opportunities and scope of jurisdiction of their occupations. Taking into consideration, the importance of castes factor, one cannot ignore the role of castes in entrepreneurship development. It matters much to assess the impact of castes and sub-castes of people on entrepreneurial development in industrial sector.

19. Planning Commission of India, New Delhi (2006)[19], stated in its reports that under the customary rules of the Hindu social order, the untouchables were denied rights to property, purse business (except polluting occupations), education and employment (excluding manual labour). The consequence of these traditional restrictions in the past are to be seen, even today in the terms of lack of ownership of agricultural land, business or non-land capital assets in education and ultimately in high incidence of poverty among them.

Report further indicates that inadequate access to agricultural land and capital leaves no option to SC workers except to resort to manual wage labour and it leads to enormously high level of manual wage labour among SC people. The argument in support of remedies against discrimination that are mainly based on historical denial of equal opportunity, due to practices of castes and untouchability based exclusion and discrimination towards untouchable and seeking provision for equal rights, safe guards against violation of equal rights and strategies for equal access or opportunities through reservation for affirmative action

Report further indicate that not only the untouchability has prevented the growth of personality of untouchables but also it comes in the way of their material well-being. The untouchability of untouchables puts constitutional fundamental rights for beyond their reach.

20. P. G. Jogdand (2008)[20] observed that, as untouchables are considered as impure and polluting.They suffer from isolation and exclusion which reflects in social and physical segregation. The comprehensive and multiple exclusion, discrimination and denial of human rights, the Dalits and untouchables have severe consequences on their overall development. Determination of occupation by birth and restrictions to change hereditary occupation and social position obviously restricts the freedom of occupation.

21. S. G. Bhanushali (2009)[21] found that, Mohammedan have excelled their performance in all the related areas of Engg. sector except marketing. Jainas are the second best in production as well as in marketing, but they are comparatively weak in financial management. Group of Parasis, Nairs and Vaish has rank third as they are doing better in creating entrepreneurs and managing well in all aspects of business. The Brahmins are strongest in marketing.

22. Surindar S. Jodhaka (2010)[22] observed that the Dalit entrepreneurs are facing many hardships due to lack of resources and caste prejudice. Despite several positive changes, caste continues to play a vital role (almost negative) in progress of them. On the other hand it is also piece of good sign that they feel proud to be in business world knowing entrepreneurs. They feel proud of the fact that, they are coming out of slavery and helping others by providing them employment opportunities.

23. Lakshmi Iyaer, (et al) (2013)[23] found that due to caste based discrimination, members of other castes do not want to work with SC entrepreneurs. SC entrepreneur lacking entrepreneurial knowledge and courage. A financial constraint also causes hurdles to SC entrepreneurs in their development.

2.3.2 Family Background and Entrepreneurship Development: Many researchers proved through their study that family background and entrepreneurship development of that particular person have certain relation with each other. Following are few findings and observations in this regard.

1. F. R. Haris (1925)[24] observed that Shri. Jamshetaji Tata laid the foundation of development of Indian Industries. Scope of his efficiency, courage and enterprising attitude was tremendous. Still then Jamshetaji Tata had to face many challenges, had to overcome many hurdles, those occurred in his mission. Healthy and supportive family background of TATA helped a lot in his entrepreneurial development.

2. J. T. Mac Crory (1956)[25] observed that, persons those who are belong to the family having inherited business and entrepreneurial background, helps in creating new entrepreneurs. It supports new generation entrepreneurs in their development process. Though it is true that the family background alone does not help the entrepreneurs in overcoming all the obstacles occurring in their business, they could survive in recession in market.However competition by the rivals, cheating or fraudulent affairs by the fellow members,technological backwardness, carelessness towards changing circumstances etc. are the factors responsible for their failure.

3. David D. Mac Clelland (1961)[26] observed that, making youth as entrepreneurs are largely depend on the family background in which they live and grow. Family atmosphere, inculcation of values, the behave of parents to the children, structure of family, efforts taken for personality development are some of the important issues on which development of the children as an entrepreneur is largely depend upon. Further Mac Clelland added that, if further scientific training is provided to the inborn and able entrepreneurs, the way of success get widen.

4. Bendix and Lipset (Ed) (1966)[27] observed that the family elements in motivation play a substantial role in the education and training of future entrepreneurs that eventually leads to social mobility. Further they observed that, it is in the family setting that the individual's motivation to achieve success in business is developed, as well as social and intellectual skills that hinders or help him in the first step along that road. This study was attempted to analyse the nexus of family variable to achievement motivation and mobility.

5. R.G. Fox (1969)[28] has studied the aspect of changes in social structure and their effects on entrepreneurship. He observed that, comparatively peoples from well known Zamindar family can easily grab the political hold and thereby they avail the economic and non-economic government aid for their entrepreneurial betterment. This helps them in achieving professional occupational success. He further found that the influencing and supportive family background of such Zamindar people contributes very much effective role in achieving their success.

6. P. Ramkrishnan (1971)[29] found that, apart from economic, technical and administrative factors, the family background, the social status of family, entrepreneurial education and training are the considerable factors those are responsible for success and failure of industries run by the entrepreneurs.

7. Z. Mars (1975)[30] observed that traditional occupation of any family, the means of production available with them and the area of entrepreneurship selected by family members are correlated with each other and these are only the factors which determines and assist in achieving the success.

8. K. L. Sharma (1975)[31] found that the entrepreneurship development is closely associated with family background, the means of production and the stage of entrepreneurial development of that particular entrepreneur. He further observed that, the entrepreneurs those are having healthy and industrial family background is certainly equipped with sufficient capital and enough self confidence in them. He further observed that entrepreneur definitely will achieve the success only if the family background of that entrepreneur is of professional industrial and healthy nature.

9. Kelly Jonathan (1978)[32] quoted his observation that a son born into high status family acquires economic resources which he then invests in education, physical capital and a like. While son from low status family gets fewer resources to invest and is consequently at disadvantage.

10. K. Ravi Chandra (1978)[33] observed that, there were some respondents acting as first generation entrepreneurs. Neither they belong to upper class society nor had they inherited progressive entrepreneurial family background with them. Despite this, they played effective role of entrepreneurs and grabbed the success.

11. G.V. Javillonar(et.al) (1987)[34] found that, industrial and occupational background of any entrepreneur is the personal and family matter of that entrepreneur, but still it is a considerable fact representing that there is a certain correlation between family background and economic support provided by the family of that particular entrepreneur. The economic help, protection and moral support provided by the family members of any industrialist or entrepreneur is held responsible for achieving height of entrepreneurial success.

12. S.M. Dahiwale (1989)[35] Observed that most of the respondents who have accepted modern jobs, reported that, their behaviour, ideology and attitude are changed positively. They are awakened from their downtrodden state of life. They are motivated by the ideologies of their Heros, the great social reformers like Chh. Shahu Raje, Mahatma Jyotirao Phule, Dr Babasaheb Ambedkar etc. and their role found to be more effective in deviating them from traditional jobs to modern jobs.

2.3.3 Social Movements and Entrepreneurship Development: Especially in the case of Scheduled Castes (SC) people, social movements led by the great social reformers have influenced immensely. Enhancement in the social and economic status through occupational mobility was possible only because of social movements in India. Following are the findings and observations in this regard:

1. Govind Gare and Shirubhau Limaye (1970)[36] conducted their study to assess the influences of movement led by Dr Babasaheb Ambedkar. Researchers observed remarkable occupational mobility among Mahar and New-Budhist. Especially, most of the Mahar and New Buddhist families gave up their traditional menial activities, and directed towards new occupations, and then followed by the Mangs, the Chambhars and the Dhor respectively.

2. Sunanda Patwardhan (1973)[37] observed that the Mahars, are the most numerous and advanced among all the SCs, because of their conversion to Buddhism in 1956. She further observed that, not a single 'Mahar' had kept up his original occupation in this urban setting. Dr Ambedkar's leadership, awakening of self respect and conversion to Buddhism are some of the important reasons for change of traditional occupations in the case of Maharas. In other two major castes i.e. Mang and Chambhar they still follow traditional occupations.

Further, on the educational transformation, a researcher found that, in urban area like Pune city, Mahars have made good progress in education as compared to other untouchable communities. On the other hand their position in rural areas is still unchanged. They are still backward educationally and economically, as compared to higher castes.

3. M. G. Kulkarni (et.al) (1975)[38] observed that, families in Chambhar and Dhor sub-castes were engaged in their traditional services as their services were reported beneficial to them. Further it was observed that Buddhist families (former Mahars) abandoned their traditional occupations and diverted towards new jobs and services as a result of their conversion to Buddhism. Some Mang families also shifted to non-traditional occupations.

4. J. V. Rahate (1985)[39] observed that, the Maharas have left their traditional occupations totally, whereas Mhetras (Scavengers) were not willing to leave their traditional job as they did not possess other alternative like educational qualification and other better means of livelihood to substitute earlier ones. Explanation given for change among the Maharas was that, due to education, they become conscious about their derogatory menial work, discarded social status, as a result of inspiration from Dr Babasaheb Ambedkar and his great social movement in upliftment of social status of untouchables in India.

5. S. M. Dahiwale (1989)[40] observed that the family background is to be as one of the contributing factors for occupational mobility. Unfavourable family background viz. economic hardship, poverty, unemployment, more depending family members etc. factors were mainly responsible for recent deviation from traditional jobs to modern jobs.

6. Uttara Shastri (1998)[41] found that the acceptance of Buddhism was mainly motivated by the desire to raise ones status. After the conversion, from Hindu ex-untouchables to Neo Buddhist,they rejected all the aspects of Hinduism, their rites, culture, festivals, Gods and Goddesses etc. However, Study further reveals that the complete negation of the old traditions have not been still possible for them.Their religious practices consists of the elements of both the pattern, traditional Hindu Mahar pattern and Buddhists pattern,

7. UNESCO Research Centre (2011)[42] found that, some inspired and motivated persons from socially and economically backward traditional society gave up their dirty and non-profitable traditional activities and accepted challenges in industrial sector by initiating new and innovating business activities and made them successful. Their strong wishes to achieving success, their education and training related to entrepreneurship, their creativeness and innovativeness was held responsible for their grand success.

2.3.4. Motivating Factors, Occupational Mobility and Entrepreneurship Development

Motivations and its intensity play a vital role in achieving great success in any field. SC entrepreneurs are motivated by many aspects and they perform their activities to achieve their goals. Following are findings and observations with regards to motivations those are held responsible to initiate and develop their enterprises.

1. F.E. Jackson (et. al) (1970)[43] observed that, the Catholics tends to come from lower occupational origin than the protestants; protestants were more likely than Catholics of the same occupational origin to enter professional and business occupations.

2. Krausz Ernest (1972)[44] observed that, 'The race' or 'colour' is being held to be the most important factor limiting the opportunities and achievement of individuals. Krausz observed in his study that, high need of achievements was the real motivational aspect of occupational mobility.

3. Sunanda Patwardhan (1973)[45] has conducted empirical study of ex-untouchables of Poona city to understand and determine the factors responsible for social and occupational mobility. She observed that ,Mahar given up traditional occupations in an urban area due to increasing literacy and higher education, along with the rejection of Hindu Social system. Chambhar and Dhor people continued to carry their hereditary profession because they viewed it was more profitable even in modern setting.

4. K. D. Gangrade (1975)[46] while analysing occupational mobility, among Chambhars and Bhangis of Chattera village in the state of Haryana, he observed that, most of the respondents were disassociated themselves from their traditional occupations. He found the strong desire to improve and attain their higher status was the most important factor contributing changes in their traditional occupation.

5. Kalam Singh (1984)[47] has investigated a phenomenon of intergenerational occupational mobility in the rural setting. In his study of six villages, he observed a tendency among the members of lower caste groups to adopt traditional occupations of higher caste groups and moved towards secular occupations.

6. Prabhakar Deshmukh (2002)[48] found that Entrepreneurship Development Programmes (EDPs) assist the persons aspiring with entrepreneurial attitude in society, for emerging themselves as successful entrepreneurs. In spite of this fact, all the persons those who participate in such a development programmes do not start their enterprises and become successful entrepreneurs, only because they are lacking proper motivation.

7. B. S. Mahind (2008)[49] observed that, majority of entrepreneurs were belongs to backward classes, both by economically and socially. Most of them had agricultural family background and had started their career at the age of sixteen, due to unemployment, but with self motivation. The finance and marketing were the most threatening problem to them.

8. Surindra S Jodhaka (2010)[50] found that the major source of motivation of SC entrepreneurs for doing new business was attaining better dignity and self respect; to have better quality of life and also to do something meaningful were the equal motivation to initiate new and innovative business.These gives them not only the income and dignity but also generate employment for other member of their community.

2.3.5 Higher Education and Entrepreneurship Development

Higher education including management, technical, vocational training programmes etc. is a key factor which provides motivational atmosphere and build the confidence. It also helps to enhance skills, traits and competencies among new and emerging entrepreneurs. Especially in case of SC entrepreneurs, following are the findings and observations reflected in various research studies.

1. S. P. Sharma (1965)[51] observed that the expenditure incurred on higher education is a fruitful investment in human resources, and such investment certainly creates good and successful entrepreneurs in society.

2. H. N. Pathak (1972)[52] found that, there is a certain positive co-relation between educational level of entrepreneur and his development at every stage.

3. S. Ashok Kumar (1974)[53] found that, entrepreneurial skills and competencies of highly educated entrepreneurs are certainly more than that of lower educated entrepreneurs.

4. Treiman, (et.al) (1975)[54] observed that, despite large differences in the educational systems, the role of educational attainment in occupational mobility is highly similar in the two countries and thus in western societies, educational attainment is found to be significant for occupational mobility.

5. N. K. Bose (1976)[55] in his study observed that occupational and social mobility is associated with the educational advancement. He further observed that having a very low proportion of literacy (1931: 4.52%), the Chamar and Mochies (leather worker) have remained in their traditional occupations in a fair numbers, where as the Kamaraj (Black Smith) having higher portion of literacy (1931:14.91%) than other artisan castes had been able to turn to other industries despite their traditional occupation was declined.

6. Kelly Jonathan (1978)[56] observed that, there is a correlation between education and occupation to be substantial in all societies but the lowest in Toro, somewhat higher in Panama, Argentina and U.S. than elsewhere.

7. Harish Doshi (1980)[57] observed that, the lack of educational ability was the main reason among some of the Bhangis and Nadias of Surat for their persuasion of conventional jobs. Harish also observed that, 72.4% of

Harijan people were engaged in non-conventional jobs, diversifying from unclean to clean work due to educational advancement in them and he found it was the positive change towards the removal of untouchability too.

8. Mumtaz Ali Khan (1980)[58] found that there is certain association of illiteracy to traditional occupations of low status and literacy beyond lower primary level to non-traditional occupations of high status.

9. R. Owen (1982)[59] observed that higher education, speed of civilisation and occupational mobility, all these three factors are correlated with each other and it helps in fostering the process of entrepreneurship development.

10. Savita Mehara, (et.al) (1984)[60] found that the upward mobility among ex untouchables of Haryana Village, as a result of expansion of education, was one of the factors responsible for deviation from own caste occupations.

11. Alexander K.C. (1988)[61] while studying the changing status of Pulaya, the Harijan of Kerala, he observed that, educational achievement was one of the determining factors for social and occupational mobility of Pulaya people in Kerala.

12. Dilip M. Sarwate (1962)[62] found that 30% entrepreneurial trainees, those who participate in entrepreneurship development programmes, could establish their enterprises, and hardly 10% amongst them remain existed after the period of 3 years from the date of their establishment as successful entrepreneurs.

13. Anjali Kurane (1997)[63] in her study observed that, so far as impact of education is concerned, most of the respondents reported that the education is necessary for getting and enhancing the business knowledge it is required to become an elite of community. It breaches the social barriers and reduces the castesm. It also helps to eradicate the superstition and blind faith.

14. J. S. Saini(1997)[64] observed that inspite of equipping themselves with necessary entrepreneurial skill, abilities, competencies' and technical knowledge through the Entrepreneurship Development Programmes, more than half of those participants and beneficiaries are failed to initiate their own enterprises.

15. Bharat Patankar (2000)[65] pointed out that with increasing commercialisation of education, the freedom to get education is already becoming meaningless, particularly for highly specialised education branches through which only rich people can be enrolled into knowledge based industries. It will also create new divisions of labourforce based on knowledge based industries. Brahmin and other upper castes will be the main beneficiaries of pure knowledge based industries and the lower range of the industries will be filled up in by Dalits.

16. Prabhakar Deshmukh (2002)[66] observed that, there are many non-economic factors which influenced the economic development of any person and that of a country. Higher education and technical education is one of them. For every person, living as a part of society need to facilitate with qualitative higher education and technical education, and also every person should always try to enhance his ability, skill and competency by utilising the same. According to him if we realize the importance of the place, role and the importance of industries in our society, and also the impact of industries on development of nation, the importance of higher and technical education taken by entrepreneurs is certainly proved. Prof Aurther Lewis, observes that there is an absence of good and quality higher education in developing and poor countries and therefore these poor countries remains poor. "(Poor nation remains poor because they lack knowledge i.e. education)".

17. B. Rajsekaran (2003)[67] observed that, development programmes in training institutes are not selective, intensive and purposeful. Financial assistance also not being provided in accordance with their efficiency.

18. K. M. Kotwal (2004)[68] conducted his study to find out correlation between entrepreneurship training and entrepreneurship development and also to find out correlation between numbers of trainees and their success ratio. He observed that despite considerable working of MCED and DIC, in Sidhudurg District, there is a less response from the beneficiaries to come forward and initiate any innovative business activity. It may be because of unawareness among present and future entrepreneurs about the schemes and programmes adopted by the DIC and MCED in Sidhudurg District.

19. R.K. Suri (et.al) (2007)[69] while elaborating the need for 'Entrepreneurial Development Programme, (EDP), authors stated that, in the past people used to believe that, 'entrepreneurs are born and not made.' It was thought that only those persons, who have got business family background can become successful entrepreneurs. According to authors, now-a-days, this view point originally invented by David Maclelland, has given place to the thinking that persons possessing proper knowledge and skill acquired through education and experiences can become successful entrepreneurs.

20. Surendar S Jodhaka (2010)[70] observed that Dalit entrepreneurs had started their enterprises prior to 1950, but during next 20 years did not seem to have been good for them.They however started to consolidate themselves after 1980. Few of them diversified themselves in to new and non-traditional occupations,like running grocery shops, restaurants, working as property dealer, school teacher etc. Virtually all of them were first generation entrepreneurs. Most of the SC entrepreneurs were admitted that education continued to be positive value in their attitude towards occupations and well being of their families.

2.3.6 Social and Political Support and Entrepreneurship Development: Social and political support is much needed factor in entrepreneurial development. Being SC people are socially suppressed and politically neglected from hundreds of years, this factor could play a major role in their entrepreneurial development.Following are few findings observed in this regard.

1. M. U. Deshpande (1964)[71] found that especially in Marathwada region all the aid and assistance provided by the government was grabbed by the high class society entrepreneurs.

2. Ransford Edward H. (et.al) (1980)[72] on the basis of Lloyed Warners study in 1941, reported that, "Lower class Black were far more disadvantaged in the socio-economic characteristics, than lower class White, and also it is mentioned that, it becomes increasingly possible for some high achieving Blacks to have greater status, in the society at larger than lower class White. These changes are noticed as a result of protective legislation in the interest of Blacks. As a result, they are entering into decision making position and also they are exercising their collective power. Further it is added that, as opportunities are increased for Blacks, some of them obtained better paying jobs and skilled blue collar and white collar positions, in United States. Due to 'Civil Right Movement', a large number of Blacks were found to be moving into high prestigious occupations, such as Business, Law, Medicine, Government and Military.

3. B. N. Kamble (1995)[73] observed that poverty and inequality get reflected in social and economic discrimination, while inequality throws the light on the class tension, poverty eradication can be advanced though the policy intervention and the programme implementation. The theories relating to the poverty explained that, there is a strong linkage with the social deprivation. Rich can save more and acquired assets and thereby dominate the political power. At the same time they can also afford the better quality of education, on the other side, the poor are facing larger demographic problems and consequently this situation perpetuates the inequality.

4. D. D. Shinde (2002)[74] while conducting his study to review the progress of Mahatma Phule Backward Class Development Corporation (MPBCDC) and to assess the impact of programmes or schemes employed by the Corporation to uplift the economic condition of SC entrepreneurs, he observed that 33% respondents did not utilise their loan given by the Corporation, for their business purpose and these have been mis-utilised, consequently, economic condition of these entrepreneurs could not improved. Researcher further observed that, respondents have no assured local market to sell their products at reasonable price on continuous basis.

5. M. Kasi Reddy (2003)[75] observed that, in India very few training programmes were conducted for SC and ST by the Government and Non Government agencies. Researcher suggested for some independent development agencies with strong financial assistance to promote the entrepreneurship among SC and ST category, in Andhra Pradesh and throughout India.

6. G. P. Kapase (2003)[76] in his religious and caste based socio-economic study reveals that, the business related occupation are found more within SC and ST communities recently due to their sound financial condition and better socio-economic development. SC and ST castes entrepreneurs are found more in numbers due to Liberal Financial Policies of Government of India.

7. Sukhdeo Thorat (2005)[77] has pointed out that discrimination on the basis of race, religion, ethnicity, national or social origin exists in many nations under diverse social, economic and political system. In order to correct the imbalance, there is a need of access to capital, assets, employment, education, political participation and to other spheres. Also needed the practices like the reservation, affirmative action, positive action or equal opportunities policies.

8. P. Y. Barute (2008)[78] While dealing with inclusive policies to be implemented for the upliftment of excluded community, found that, the economic and non-economic support provided them by the Government to these people are misappropriated or mis-utilised for wrong use. Banking and Financial institutions are not assisting, on priority basis to Dalit Self

Help Group and entrepreneurs engaged in entrepreneurial activities. Education and Training at all level are not available so as to enhance the skills, competencies and capabilities of SC entrepreneurs to explore their employment potentials.

9. Bharatiya shishu Evom Mahila Vividh Vikas Samiti, New Delhi, (2009)[79] has conducted research to identify the key variables responsible for the emergence of the entrepreneurship, their circumstances and conditions, their level of success and the constraints or challenges those typically faced by SC entrepreneurs in the state of Bihar, Maharashtra, Panjab, West Bangal and Uttar Pardesh. It was reported that they chose entrepreneurship by default or for negative reasons such as their inability to get a job. Almost half of the respondents attributed their failure to the intensity of competition and lack of social support. 76% respondents reported that they found difficult to get help from funding agencies. It was further found that the training programmes need to focus not just on providing technical skills in a vocation, but also cover the general principles of business management.

10. Chandrapal (2010)[80] has prepared and published report on "Action Points" to be taken for the development of Schedule Caste and Schedule Tribes community in India. In his report he observed that the participation of SC and ST people in trade, commerce and industry is negligible due to lack of adequate finance to be provided by the State and National Financial Institutions and the Banks. Therefore it is imperative to reserve 25% of total loan advanced for SC and ST community for the economic development and participation in all the above activities. Further author expected that, all-round efforts are needed to ensure to make SC and ST small entrepreneurs. The debts equity ratio and collateral guarantee condition need to be relaxed.

11. Surindar S. Jodhaka (2010)[81] found that despite all adverse facts and circumstances, it is found that Dalit entrepreneurs are finding their space and position in entrepreneurial world. Due to success in business, they found much easier to enter into main stream of political space, but not into a social and cultural space. However, success in politics (especially in UP state) helped Dalit entrepreneurs worked as shield in their business and individual sphere of life. Further it is observed that, Dalit entrepreneurs are facing many hardships due to lack of resources and caste prejudice. Despite several positive changes, caste continues to play a vital role (almost negative) in progress of them. On the other hand it is also piece of good sign that they feel proud to be in business enterprise knowing as entrepreneurs. They feel proud of the fact that, they are coming out of slavery and helping others by providing them employment.

12. CII (2011)[82] in its report reveled Forbes Marshell Pvt. Ltd is a Pune based process efficiency and energy conservation company, has undertaken an Affirmative Action for SC and ST candidates by encouraging and mentoring them for setting up their new enterprises, in turns which becomes, supplier to the Forbes Marshell Company. In this case study report it is found that, though SCs and STs formed a quarter of the country's population, they accounted for only a marginalised fraction of India's work force. According to Mr. Forbes, affirmative action, is the appropriate way to include inclusive growth for the country and he also believes that once affirmative action is adopted voluntarily, diversity will become a part of India's business fabric.

13. Lakshmi Iyaer, (et al) (2013)[83] observed that political gains have not manifested to the SC and ST entrepreneurs to the required extent. The rise of Dalit Millionaires driven in past by newer economic freedom does not appear representative of the broader swathes of SC/ST population at least until 2005. The growth of enterprises depends upon strong network effects for finding the right worker and for making links with suppliers and customers. SC and ST entrepreneurs are might be disadvantaged by their relatively smaller network.

14. S. Ananth (et.al) (2013)[84] found that without paradigm shift, especially on the part of banks, financial inclusion is bound to fall short of expectations. The banking sector should look at effort to expand inclusions not as capital cost or as charitable expenses, but as a long term investment in the future. The soundness of such investment is to be borne out in the success of individual business.

2.3.7 Globalisation and Entrepreneurship Development: Globalisation is the ultimate result of free economic policies adopted by the countries all over the world. Uncontrolled business activities across the globe have been provided many opportunities for entrepreneurial development and some unavailable threats and challenges before entrepreneurs. Following are the observations with regards to SC entrepreneurs about the globalisation.

1. Kumar Raj (2000)[85] observed that Dalit needs globalisation because they want to be a part of the mainstream of economic development. He points out that, Dalit wants openness because their rich cultural heritage has been submerged. The globalisation will help them to come out of the forced cultural silence and speak to the world. He further found that, Dalits are not against globalisation, what they opposed to be the fact that national policy which ignore the basic needs of poor Dalits.

2. Bharat Patankar (2000)[86] has observed that the caste system and its characteristics has relevance to capitalism and liberalisation. According to his observation, today's capitalist class is formed out of old castes and communities like Brahmin, Banias, Kshatriya, Kayyasthas, Parasis, and the hierarchy within the capitalist class and exploiting classes are determined mainly by their castes origin. He further found that new industries based knowledge and information and development of R and D units of various industrial houses, the majority of Dalits, despite reservations, scholarships have remained a part of unorganised sector.

3. S. K. Thorat (2002)[87] found that the new economic policy proved to be harmful to Dalits and poor in the terms of rise in poverty, unemployment and caste-based market discrimination.

4. R.M. Sarkar (2006)[88] found that, the globalisation is the central driving force that is reshaping modern societies and world orders and no society escape from its reach, as it recasts traditional patterns, creates new hierarchies and the most of crucially reshaped the power functioning authority and the goals of national government. He further found that the globalisation has made an adverse impaction the all social groups which have already been pushed down by centuries of oppression. According to him, since the last one decade, the livelihood of Dalit communities has become miserable.

5. D. C. Kirtiraj (2007)[89] while studying occupational patterns of respondents, observed that, majority of respondents employed in agriculture and allied sectors, have perceived higher impact of globalisation. He further found that the impact of globalisation was likely to vary with occupational pattern of respondents,

6. Lakshmi Iyaer, (et al) (2013)[90]observed that lower castes have risen in Indian politics and rapid economic development of India, especially after opening of the economy to foreign goods and capital, liberating the economic activities within the country in the mid 1980's. They further observed that not all sections of society have benefited equally from economic growth, due to steadily rising inequality in the last decade. On the contrary rich have benefited more than the poor and likewise upper caste are benefited more than the lower castes (Dalits).

2.4 Conclusion

In this chapter, review of existing research activities have been taken purposefully for knowing present status of all the business environmental issues and its impact on entrepreneurship development especially among marginalised communities. All the findings and the observations of researchers in this field proves marginally that the business environmental issues like social, religious, political, occupational, cultural, economic, educational, motivational etc. and entrepreneurship development are closely associated and dependent on each other. Due to adverse socio-economic background, SC entrepreneurs are facing difficulties in the way of their development.Constitutional measures and government efforts of course especially since the decade of 1980 have been giving positive support in entrepreneurship development among this category cannot be overlooked.

References

1. H.A. Milman (1954), The Marwadi; A Study of Group of Trading Castes, Unpublished M.A. Thesis of University of California, Berkeley.
2. Max Webber (1958), Effects on Castes and Sub-castes on Entrepreneurship Talcott Pearsons, Charles Scribner's Sons, New York, pp. 17 To 52.
3. J. J. Barna (1960), Industrial Entrepreneurship in Madras States, Asia Publishing House Bombay,
4. R. Madhavan (Jan 28 Feb 4, 1963), Pattern of Enterprises of Chattiare, In Malaya, 1880 To 1930, Economic and Political Weekly Vol. 13, pp. 146 To 154.
5. M.U. Deshpande (1964), Entrepreneurship of Small Scale Industries," Deep and Deep Publication, New Delhi. pp. 282.
6. Ito Shoji (Sept 1966), A Note on Business Combine In India, Special Reference to Nathi Kotti Chettaiare, In Developing Economy, Vol. IV, 3, pp. 367 To 380.
7. Liberson S. and Fuguilt G.V. (September 1967), Negro- White Occupational Differences In The Absence of Discrimination, American Journal of Sociology, Vol. 73 No. 2, p. 197 and 198 quoted by S.M. Dahiwale in Emerging Entrepreneurship Among Scheduled Castes.
8. Almendu Guha (29th Aug. 1970), Parasi Seths and Entrepreneurs, Economic and Political Weekly Vol. V, p. 35.
9. John Kunkel (1970), Society and Economic Growth: A Behavioral Perspective of Social Changes, Oxford University Press London, pp. 260-270, quoted by Dr Prabhakar Deshmukh, Udyojakta Vikas Pipalapure Prakashan Nagpur, 2002.
10. B.S. Bhatia(1974), New Industrial Entrepreneurs, Their Origin and Problems, Journal of General Management. Vol. 2, pp. 69 To 79.
11. E.W. Nafzigar (Jan 1975), Class, Caste and Community of South India Industrialist; an Examination of Horatio Alger Model In the Journal of Development Studies Vol. II, pp. 131 To 148.

12. G.S. Ghurye (1978), Caste, Class and Occupation, Popular Book Depot. Mumbai., p. 142, quoted by V. N. Gajendragadkar, Castes, Races in India.
13. R.A. Sharma (1980), Entrepreneurial Changes is Indian Industries, Sterling Publishers, New Delhi,
14. S. M. Dahiwale (1989), Emerging Entrepreneurship among Scheduled Castes, Research Thesis submitted to Shivaji University Kolhapur,
15. Dr B.R.Ambedkar's (1989),Writing and Speeches Vol. 5, Vol.7, Government of Maharashtra.
16. D. P. Pandit (1995), Creative Response in Indian Economy; A Regional Analysis, the Economic Weekly, Vol. IX No 8 and 9, pp. 283 to 286 and 315 to 317.
17. D. Narendra Kumar (1995), Entrepreneurship In Small Scale Sector, Discovery Publishing House, New Delhi, pp. 150 To 161.
18. Prabhakar Deshmukh (June 2002), Udyojakata Vikas: Sankalpana Ani Vyavhar, Pimpalapure and Co. Nagpur, Page 216 to 245.
19. Planning Commission of India (2006), New Delhi General Guidelines for Formulation, Implementation and Monitoring of Schedule Caste Sub Plan (SCSP) For States and Central Ministry Department, pp. 9 to 15.
20. Prof. P.G. Jogdand (March 2008), Understanding Social Exclusion and Discrimination: A Sociological Perspective, A Seminar Paper Presented at International Seminar on Social Exclusion and Inclusive Policies in South Asia. Organised by Shivaji University Kolhapur.
21. S.G.Bhanushali (2009), Entrepreneurial Development in Engg. Industry in Kolhapur City. Ph.D Thesis submitted to Shivaji University, Kolhapur.
22. Surindar S. Jodhaka (Nov. 2010), Dalits In Business; Self Employed Scheduled Castes in North-west India, Working Paper Series Vol. IV, By Indian Institute of Dalit Studies.
23. Lakshmi Iyaer, Tarun khanna, Asutosh Varshney (Feb 9, 2013), Caste and Entrepreneurship in India; Economic and Political Weekly, Vol. XLVII, pp. 52 to 59.
24. F.R., Haris (1925) J.N.Tata: A Chronicle of His Life", Oxford University Press, London.
25 J.T. Mac Crory (1956), Small Industrialists in North Indian Towns. A Case Study in Latest Industrial Potential, Ministry of Comm. and Industries Government India.
26. David D. Mac Clelland (1961), The Achieving Society, The Free Press Journal, New York.
27. Bendix and Lipset (Ed) (1966), Class, Status And Power, Free Press Journal, pp. 591 To 601 quoted by S.M. Dahiwale in Emerging Entrepreneurship Among Scheduled Castes.
28. R.G. Fox (1969), From Zamindar to Ballot Box, Cornell University Press, New York.
29. P. Ramkrishnan (July 1971), New Entrepreneurship in Small Scale Industries in New Delhi, Economics And Scientific Research Foundation, New Delhi, p. 27.

30. Z. Mars (1975), Assistance to Small Scale Industries in Kerala, an Indian Case, In Development of Changes Vol. XVI, pp. 14 to 18.
31. K. L. Sharma (1975), Entrepreneurial Performance in Role Perspective, Abhinav Publication, New Delhi.
32. Kelly Jonathan (March 1978), Wealth and Family Background in the Occupational Career, The British Journal of Sociology, Vol. 29, pp. 98 to 106 quoted by S.M. Dahiwale in Emerging Entrepreneurship Among Scheduled Castes.
33. K. Ravi Chandra (1978), An Entrepreneurial Success; A Psychological Study, in Hyderabad City of Andhra Pradesh.
34. G.V. Javillonar and G.R. Peters (1987), Sociological and Psychological Aspects of Indian Entrepreneurship, The British Journal of Sociology, Vol. 24, pp. 314-328.
35. S. M. Dahiwale (1989), Emerging Entrepreneurship among Scheduled Castes, Research thesis submitted to Shivaji University Kolhapur.
36. Govind Gare and Shirubhau Limaye (1970), Maharashtratil Dalit – Shodh Anni Bodh" (Marathi), Sahadhya Prakashan, Mumbai, pp. 68 to 166.
37. Sunanda Patwardhan (1965), A Study of Scheduled Castes in an Urban Setting, A Ph.D. thesis, submitted to Pune University.
38. M.G. Kulkarni and A.B. Hiramani(Sept. 1975) Occupational Pattern, In Two Marathwada Villages; A Comparative Study, University Journal Vol. – XIV, Page 93 To 97.
39. J. V. Rahate (1985), Modernisation among Scheduled Caste, With Special Reference to Maharas, Weavers and Sweepers of Nagpur City; Ph.D. Thesis submitted to Marathwada University Aurangabad, Page 188 To 198.
40. S. M. Dahiwale (1989), Emerging Entrepreneurship among Scheduled Castes, Research thesis submitted to Shivaji University Kolhapur.
41. Uttara Shastri (1998), Neo Buddhists: As Marginal Group in India, – Ph.D. thesis Submitted to Pune University.
42. UNESCO Research Centre (2011), Social Aspects of Small Industries In India, Studied In Hawarth and Bombay, UNESCO Research Centre on Social and Economic Development In Southern Asia, New Delhi.
43. F.E Jackson; W.S. Fox and CroulettJr. (1970), Religion and Occupational Achievement, American Sociological Review, Vol. 35, pp. 51 To 60.
44. Krausz Ernest (1972), Factors of Social Mobility in British Minority Groups, The British Journal of Sociology Vol. 23, p. 272 to 283 quoted by S.M. Dahiwale in Emerging Entrepreneurship Among Scheduled Castes.
45. Sunanda Patwardhan (1973), Changes among India's Harijans, Orient Longman Publications, Page 203.
46. K.D. Gangurde (Sept.1975), Social Mobility in India, a Study of Depressed Class, Men in India, Vol. No. 53, Page 252.
47. Kalam Singh (1984), Occupational Mobility in Rural Setting, The Indian Journal of Social Research, Vol. 25.

48. Prabhakar Deshmukh (June 2002), Udyojakata Vikas: Sankalpana Ani Vyavhar, Pimpalapure and Co. Nagpur, Page 216 to 245.
49. B.S. Mahind (2008), A Study of Entrepreneurship Development In Khanapur, Vita Town in Sangli District. Ph.D thesis submitted to Shivaji University, Kolhapur.
50. Surindar S. Jodhaka (2010), Dalits in Business; Self Employed Scheduled Castes In North-west India, Working paper series Vol. IV, Indian Institute of Dalit Studies, New Delhi.
51. S.P. Sharma (Dec.1965), Emergence of Industrial Entrepreneur: A Sociological Process, In Indian Journal of Commerce, Vol. Xiii, Part iv N.65, pp. 369-373.
52. H. N. Pathak (Nov. 1972), The Entrepreneurs Technician and Managers, In Small Scale Units, Economic and Political Weekly, Review of Management Vol. VII, pp. 179-187.
53. S. Ashok Kumar (1974), Entrepreneurship in Small Industry, Discovery Publishing House, New Delhi. Page 43.
54. Treiman, Donald J and Terrel Kermit (1975), The Process of Status Attainment in the United States And Great Britain, American Journal of Sociology. Vol. 81, p. 579 quoted by S.M. Dahiwale in Emerging Entrepreneurship Among Scheduled Castes.
55. N. K. Bose(1976), The Structure of Hindu Society, (Trans) Sangam Books, p. 51 quoted by S.M. Dahiwale in Emerging Entrepreneurship Among Scheduled Castes.
56. Kelly Jonathan (March 1978), Wealth and Family Background in the Occupational Career, The British Journal Of Sociology, Vol. 29, pp. 98 To 106 quoted by S.M. Dahiwale in Emerging Entrepreneurship Among Scheduled Castes.
57. Harish Doshi (1980), Occupational Diversification and Removal of Untouchability, Gujarat University, Ahamdabad.
58. Mumtaz Ali Khan (1980), Scheduled Castes and Their Status in India, Uppal Publication House, New Dehli, Page 127 to 128.
59. R. Owen (1982), Peasant Entrepreneurs in Industrial City in Singer M (Ed), pp. 133 to 166.
60. Savita Mehara (et al) (1984), Changing Correspondence Between Castes and Occupation; A Socio-Economic Analysis, The Eastern Anthropologist Vol. 37, p. 335.
61. K.C. Alexander (July 1988), Changing Status of Pulayas, Harijan of Kerala, Economic and Political weekly, Page 321. Quoted by S.M. Dahiwale in Emerging Entrepreneurship Among Scheduled Castes.
62. Dilip M.Sarwate (1988), Entrepreneurial Development: Concept and Practices, Everest Publishing House, Pune, p. 67.
63. Anjali Kurane (April 1997), Ethnic Identity and Social Mobility; A Case study of Buddhists in Pune, Ph. D Thesis Submitted to Pune University.
64. J.S Saini (1997), Entrepreneurship Development Programmes and Its Practices, Deep and Deep Publications, New Delhi, pp. 200-339.

65. Bharat Patankar (2000), New Economic Policy and Dalit: Alternatives of Development, P.G. Jogdand (ed), pp. 58 to 67.
66. Prabhakar Deshmukh (June 2002), Udyojakata Vikas: Sankalpana Ani Vyavhar, Pimpalapure and Co. Nagpur, Page 216 to 245.
67. B. Rajsekaran Entrepreneurial Performance (4 Dec 2003), SEDEME Vol. 30, pp. 10 to 13.
68. K.M. Kotwal (Dec.2004), Role of MCED and DIC in Entrepreneurship Development, In Sindhudurg District. M. Phil Dissertation submitted to Shivaji University, Kolhapur,
69. R.K. Suri and Sharma (2007), Entrepreneurship Development, Kitab Mahal Publications, pp. 301 to 315.
70. Surindar S. Jodhaka (2010), Dalits in Business; Self Employed Scheduled Castes In North-west India, Working paper series Vol. IV, Indian Institute of Dalit Studies, New Delhi.
71. M.U. Deshpande (1964), Entrepreneurship of Small Scale Industries," Deep and Deep Publication, New Delhi. pp. 282.
72. Ransford Edward H. And Jeffries Vincent (1980), Social Stratification – A Multiple Hierarchy Approach, Allyn Bacon, pp. 156 to 174 quoted by S.M. Dahiwale in Emerging Entrepreneurship Among Scheduled Castes.
73. B.N. Kamble(1995), Effectiveness of Developmental Programmes for SC and ST In Maharashtra. A Ph.D. thesis, submitted to Pune University.
74. D.D. Shinde (2002), Role of Mahatma Phule Backward Class Development Corporation, In Economic Upliftment of SC Community, A Case Study of Kolhapur City. M. Phil Dissertation submitted to Shivaji University, Kolhapur.
75. M. Kasi Reddy (Jan-Mar 2003), Entrepreneurial Process among SCs and STs In Andhra Pradesh, The Indian Journal of Commerce Vol. 56, pp. 83 To 87.
76. G.P. Kapase (2003), An analytical study of Woman Entrepreneurship in Marathwada Ph.D. thesis submitted to Shivaji University, Kolhapur.
77. Sukhdeo Thorat (May 2005), why Reservation in Private Sector is Necessary, A Seminar Paper Presented in the International Conference, Hydrabad pp. 30-35.
78. Prakash Yashwant Burute (March 2008), Views of Dr Babasaheb Ambedkar on Social Exclusion and Inclusive Policy Social Exclusions And Inclusive Policies In South Asia At Shivaji University, Kolhapur.
79. Bharatiya Shishu Evom Mahila Vividh Vikas Samiti (2009-10), New Delhi, Researcher Study on Entrepreneurial Challenge for SC Persons In India Sponsored and Funded By Planning Commission Government of India New Delhi, pp. 18 to 70.
80. Chandrapal (2010) (Adviser, Planning, Commission, Government of India, New Delhi) Action Point for Development of Schedule Castes and Schedule Tribes pp. 9 To 15.
81. Surindar S. Jodhaka (2010), Dalits in Business; Self Employed Scheduled Castes In North-west India, Working paper series Vol. IV, Indian Institute of Dalit Studies, New Delhi.

82. CII (2011), A Report on Affirmative Action, With Reference to Forbs Marshell Pvt. Ltd.: A case study.
83. Lakshmi Iyacr (Feb. 9, 2013), Tarun khanna, Asutosh Varshney, Caste and Entrepreneurship in India; Economic and Political Weekly, Vol. XLVII, pp. 52 to 59.
84. S. Ananth, T. Sabri OnCu (Feb. 16, 2013), Challenges to Financial Inclusion in India, The case study of Andhra pradesh, Economic and Political Weekly, Vol. XLVIII, p. 77.
85. Kumar Raj (2000), Article on Globalisation and Dalit Culture, P.G. Jogdand (ed). pp. 89-90.
86. Bharat Patankar (2000), New Economic Policy and Dalit: Alternatives of Development, P.G. Jogdand (ed) pp. 58 to 67.
87. S.K. Thorat (2002), Ambedkars Economic Ideas and liberalisation: Emerging Challenges before Dalit. 100 years of Reservation, An Appraisal and Assessment, under the ages of Republican Party of India, Hyderabad (AP),
88. R.M. Sarkar (2006), Dalits in India – Past and Present, Serial Publications Delhi (ed).
89. D.C. Kirtiraj (October 2007), Study of Impact of Globalisation on Socio-economic status of Neo-Buddhist Community in Akola District., Ph.D. thesis submitted to Pune University.
90. Lakshmi Iyaer, Tarun khanna, Asutosh Varshney (Feb 9, 2013), Caste and Entrepreneurship in India; Economic and Political Weekly, Vol. XLVII, pp. 52 to 59.

Chapter - III

Entrepreneurship Development Programme (EDP)

3.1 Introduction

According to Peter Drucker, a well known management expert, an entrepreneur is a person who always searches for change, responds to it and exploit it as an opportunities with his innovative approaches. He undertakes an economic activity which involves reasonable risk by making investment under the conditions of uncertainty,he plans, organises, controls his entrepreneurial activity and takes decisions so as to increase his production, productivity and profit.

Entrepreneurship development is a complex phenomenon. It is an essential ingredient of economic development, in achieving the goals of all round development of any country as well as any business organisation. Consequently many entrepreneurial opportunities are emerged in various fields of manufacturing, trading and service rendering activities. Such opportunities, however are more perceptible to an emerging entrepreneur, if they are exposed to the latest development in respective filed. Easy access and understanding of information widens the scope of opportunity available to such entrepreneur.

3.2 Significance of Entrepreneurship Development Programmes (EDPs)

It is well known fact that, an entrepreneur not necessarily born, he can be developed. The development of an entrepreneur occurs by accumulating the relevant skills, traits, competencies, know how, experiences and contacts over the periods. It requires mega treatment of self development at least for ten to fifteen years.

Though entrepreneurship is born with certain domestic intelligence and flair for creating energetic innovation,such intelligence and talent is required to be sharpen with the help of systematic and scientific planned programme with precise curriculum so as to strengthen his entrepreneurial motive as well as to acquire necessary skills and capabilities for playing his entrepreneurial role effectively. Entrepreneurship Development Programme is utmost important,especially for the emerging entrepreneurs in SC category, those who wish to give up their unhygienic, dead end and low paying occupations and opt for innovative, highly paid and respectful business opportunities.

3.3 Objectives of Entrepreneurship Development Programme

Entrepreneurship Development Programme (EDP) may be conducted in the light of following objectives.

1. To develop entrepreneurial skills, traits and competencies among emerging entrepreneurs.
2. To upgrade the awareness, with regards to technical know-how and techniques about existing as well as new and innovative entrepreneurial opportunities.
3. To create supportive environment especially in rural and semi-urban area to stimulate new business organisations and to encourage for expansion of existing business activities.
4. To generate self employment and job opportunities to unemployed youth.
5. To promote the small and medium business enterprises in the light of national programme and policies.
6. To enhance and consolidate the socio-economic and entrepreneurial status of emerging entrepreneurs in non-business communities.
7. To divert more people especially women and excluded community people towards non-traditional and modern business opportunities.
8. To understand the process and procedure of setting up of business.
9. To understand and develop entrepreneurial culture so as to take right decision at right time.
10. To accelerate the process of entrepreneurial and economic development.

3.4 Areas of Entrepreneurship Development Programme

Entrepreneurship development is a complex phenomenon. It involves various training and motivation development programmes with planned syllabi and pre-determined objectives to be achieved by the candidate. In a country like India, where human resources are found abundantly, needy and enthusiastic individuals in all segments of society can be identified, motivated and trained them through proper Entrepreneurial Development programmes (EDPs) for undertaking ventures with moderate risk.

Following are the important areas in which Entrepreneurship Development Programme may be conducted.

3.4.1 Entrepreneurship Awareness Training Programme: Entrepreneurship has opened new avenues and opportunities in different sector of economy on the background of globalisation, especially for the non-business community people in India. In Entrepreneurship Development Programmes (EDPs), adequate awareness is made among first generation entrepreneurs about possible opportunities to start micro and small business enterprises within the region. Training is given to search an ideas related to business and also guidance is given to transform those ideas into business opportunities. It also involves identification of possible problems in establishing and running the business successfully.

3.4.2 Industrial Motivation Training Programme: This training programme is aimed at inculcating the aspiration of initiating new and innovative business or conducting the existing business with new and innovative way. This training programme is also aimed at increasing the participant's level of success and confidence by developing right attitude and behaviour towards their business.

3.4.3 Product Oriented Entrepreneurship Development Training Programme: For making more purposeful 'Entrepreneurship Development Programme' proper direction and training is given with respect to manufacturing of goods and services. In this type of training,availability and nature of raw material, manpower, electricity and fuel resources, techniques and process of production, marketing etc. issues are taken into consideration.Attempts are to be made for practicing product oriented training so as to solve operational problems likely to be occur in future.

3.4.4 Skill Development Training Programme: Entrepreneurship Development Programme itself is a Skill Development Programme, organised for all kinds of entrepreneurs to develop their skills, traits and competencies. Skill development is a core aspect of any entrepreneurship development programme, as it improve their ability to perform functions those are related to attaining the goal.

In this type of training programme, attempts are made to develop both kinds of skills viz soft skills like problem solving, leadership, ethical behaviour, open mindness, persuasiveness, communication, sense of responsibilities, creativeness and innovativeness etc. and hard skills like technological ability, ability to organise, network building, management style, ability to manage the change, ability to work hard, ability of documentation and presentation,etc.

3.4.5 Management Development Training Programme: This type of training programme is organised with an object of developing managerial qualities among candidates under training like planning,organising, co-ordinating, staffing, controlling, directing, decisionmaking negotiating, motivating, budgeting etc. abilities those are essentially required for making business organisation successful. Appropriate guidance is also given to the trainees to make the use of these qualities under different circumstances in different atmosphere.

3.4.6 Target Group Oriented Entrepreneurship Development Training Programme

This is the unique and specialised training programme organised for the trainees according to the need of different target groups, viz,trading entrepreneurs, industrial entrepreneurs, agricultural entrepreneurs, service provider entrepreneurs, technical entrepreneurs, non-technical entrepreneurs, motivated entrepreneurs, induced entrepreneurs, rural entrepreneurs, urban and semi-urban entrepreneurs, male entrepreneurs, female entrepreneurs etc. Separate training is given to each individual group of entrepreneurs as they require different types of skills and abilities from each other group.

3.5 Stages in Entrepreneurship Development Programme

Entrepreneurship Development Programme (EDP) is an effective tool designed and applied for developing human resource. This programme is conducted with the planned syllabi, under the guidance and supervision of experts.Especially for the first generation entrepreneurs, who cannot initiate and conduct business enterprises successfully at their own, EDP plays significant role in strengthening their entrepreneurial motivation and behaviour. It also helps to acquire new skills and traits and build the competencies in them. Precise and need based planning of EDP, selection of proposed entrepreneurs, seriously execution of programmes, techniques and methodology used for imparting the training, devoted participation of candidates and achievement of the aims and objectives of training are the most essential parts of consideration while conducting EDP. Generally, Entrepreneurship Development Programme is based on three tiered approaches with three distinct stages. Every individual approach has its own object and it is achieved with different activities. These are as follow:

3.5.1. *Initial Stage:* Creating Awareness and Identification of Potential: This is the first and the most important stage of EDP, in which focus is given on providing positive motivation and strengthening the behavioural aspects of participants. Participants are induced to think and understand why one should be an entrepreneur and what are the needed inputs for becoming successful entrepreneur. In this stage, careful attention is given on identification of existing entrepreneurial abilities with scientific method, among the participants. Entrepreneurial opportunities are discussed and indentified with thorough discussion. Initial guidance and support is provided for selecting the products,preparation of project reports, availing the required finance, technology to be availed and used in manufacturing process, marketing of products etc. Positive motivation and behavioural aspects of them are strengthened, and finally basic entrepreneurial training is provided so as to initiate business enterprise independently.

3.5.2. *Development Stage:* Supporting for Establishing and Developing Enterprises: In this second stage of entrepreneurship development process, actual help and support is given while establishing an enterprise and developing it as successful business unit. For this purpose guidance for registration of business enterprise is provided. Guidance and help is extended for availing infrastructural facilities, raising finance, recruiting manpower, supporting in operational activities, marketing the products etc. Management consultancy services and updated information is provided as per demand.

3.5.3. *Sustaining Stage:* Making Capacity Building Efforts:In this third and final stage, additional help and support is provided to individual entrepreneur for strengthening his capacity and capability. Attempts are made to upgrade his existing skills and techniques periodically. Guidance and help is extended for additional capacity utilisation. Help through the State Policies, Government and Semi Government Organisations, Non Government Agencies is provided. Purposeful focus is given on developing the innovations and innovative approaches in them. Quality testing and improving services, diagnostic industrial and extension services are also provides to the entrepreneurs participated in entrepreneurship development programme.

3.6 Characteristics of Successful Entrepreneur

Successful entrepreneur is usually indentified with certain characteristics with which he performs his activities and attains the ultimate results in the form of success. Following are the expected essential characteristics of successful entrepreneur.

3.6.1. Innovator: Innovativeness is an attitude of a person doing something new or in a different way. Here, entrepreneur is consistently expected to perform his activities with new and innovative approaches. His innovativeness always bring fruitful results for himself as well as for his customer and all other stakeholders.

3.6.2. Risk Bearer: Entrepreneurship is an attitude of mind which calls for calculated risk. Being entrepreneur is innovator, and doing something new or in a different way, he is expected to bear moderate risk. In any business, as such, there is always risk of incurring losses due to many reasons like tough competition, change in Government's policies, adoption of new technology, customers likes and dislikes, change in climatic conditions etc. Inspite of this, entrepreneur need to come forward with positive state of mind and carry his business. Despite his failure once or twice, he should not give up his hopes of success in near future.

3.6.3. Decision Maker: Decision making is an ability to take right decision at right time. While establishing, organising and running the business enterprise, an entrepreneur takes many important decisions. His ultimate success or failure is mostly depending upon his decision making ability which is attained through experiences, education and knowledge. It can be gained also by seeking guidance of seniors and experts.

3.6.4. Problem Solver: There are many problems those usually occur in the process of entrepreneurship.Successful entrepreneur with his forecasting ability,assess such possible problems well in advance. Related information and data is gathered systematically. It is analysed scientifically, sometimes with the help of laboratory. Conclusions are drawn accurately and thus problems are converted into opportunities. While solving the problems, sometimes consultation is made with the experts and senior experienced persons and appropriate measures are taken accordingly.

3.6.5. Opportunity Seeker: Entrepreneurship, itself is a opportunity seeking process.In the very beginning, an entrepreneur use to search an opportunities of starting new business. Of course initiating of such new business mostly depend up on his motivations, aspirations,level and quality of education, socio-economic support and his family backdrop. Never the less indentifying and trapping right opportunity and converting it into success is one of the significant character of successful entrepreneur.

3.6.6. Ideal Leader: Successful entrepreneur possess the character of true leader. While leading his team of colleague, he motivates them properly, initiate the confidence in them, seeks their positive feedback, clarify them priorities, supports them morally and economically for advancement and divert them positively towards achieving predetermined goals.

3.6.7. Society Caretaker: An entrepreneur himself is an integral part of society and social atmosphere. Values, thoughts and culture of society are utmost important for him and for his business. Real entrepreneur never takes undue advantage of social and economic conditions arises in society for his own benefit at the cost of well-being of the society at large. He is always in search of innovative methods and approaches for producing quality products for his customers with minimum possible price. His business activities are directed towards achieving social goals on larger interest. His employment generation work is a great relief to the society where large number of peoples are unemployed.

3.6.8. Dreamer and Creator: According to Robert D. Hisrich, entrepreneur is a person who dreams great dreams. Real entrepreneur dreams to establish successful new business venture, to earn wealth as well as name and fame. He visualises his dream project, work hard consistently, removes all the obstacles and brings his dream into existence. His creative, hardworking nature and positive state of mind works together for making his dream true.

3.6.9. Planner,Organiser and Administrator: An entrepreneur is a good planner. He plans his all the activities clearly and firmly, in accordance with the objectives of his business organisation.He is also good organiser of land, labour, capital, technology, instruments, machines and all other assets those are essentially, required for running the business effectively and efficiently. He administers all the activities fruitfully leading to words attainment of goals and objectives.

3.7. Qualities of Successful Entrepreneurs

Generally, there are two types qualities observed among successful entrepreneurs. First types of qualities are known as personal qualities and other types of qualities are known as functional qualities. These qualities are explained in brief as follows.

3.7.1. Personal Qualities: Personal qualities are associated with an individual entrepreneur, as an integral part of his personality. These are found differently from person to person. Major personal qualities are:

1. **Vision:** Vision means keen foresight to predict the future business environment, likely changes in market, customers' attitude, technological developments, government's policies etc.
2. **Motivation:** Motivation is an inner urge, drives, desire, aspirations, striving or needs that direct, control or explain the behaviour of entrepreneur.
3. **Dynamism:** It is an ability to create dynamic and energetic environment at work place. This positive and conducive atmosphere helps leader and his followers to act together positively in achieving aims and objectives of an organisation within stipulated time and with lesser cost.
4. **Mental Ability:** Mental Ability involves intelligence and analysing ability of an entrepreneur in different situations and different environmental conditions. It requires knowledge, experience and creative thinking ability.
5. **Flexible:** It is an ability to adjust with different situations and different people involved in business activities. It is also way of adopting convenient alternative to overcome adverse situation.
6. **Determination:** It means decision making ability of an entrepreneur. It involves determination of goals and objectives, sources and adequacy of capital, human resources, use of technology, method of production and marketing etc.
7. **Optimist:** It means positive state of mind irrespective of any kind of situation and hoping for success rather than experiencing failure. It also refers as strong will power of riding over adverse situation and conquer the battle of struggle.
8. **Self Confident:** It is a capacity to believe in own ability and strength having full faith on own knowledge, skills and competencies.
9. **Commitment:**Commitment means deep sense of desire or strong wish to complete particular task within stipulated time. It is time bound assignment fulfilling as a moral binding irrespective of any sacrifice at any cost to be paid for.

10. **Hungry for Success:** It means, always looking for big success and high achievements, may be in the form of money, wealth, status, name, fame, self satisfaction, social betterment etc.

3.7.2 Functional Qualities

Functional qualities are attained through the purposeful training or through the experiences in performing entrepreneurial activities over the years. These types of qualities need to be developed intentionally which ultimately helps in enhancing the capability of an entrepreneur. Major functional qualities are:

1. **Innovation:** Innovation is a spark of change that ignites improvement and progress in the stage of things. The process of innovation involves, converting concepts in to realities.The essence of innovation is putting new, high valves and ideas in to action.
2. **Strategic Planning and Organising:** is an ability to evolve relevant strategy aimed at safeguarding and promoting the interest of organisation. organising means generating all the resources those are required to establish an organisation.
3. **Risk Bearing:** It is an ability to take calculated risk while planning and performing the business activities. It is not simply the attitude of depending upon chance factor to get expected results but to put an honest effort to set desired result.
4. **Creativity:** It refers to the intellectual power creating something new and innovative things rather than imitating something which already exists.
5. **Adoptiveness:** It means willing to adopt change, if situation demands, believing that the journey of change is not without its obstacles, but it is also with full of opportunities and rewards.
6. **Quality Consciousness:** It means setting high quality standards for one self and put in his best for achieving these standards. Believing in the excellence which is reflected in every thing he does.
7. **Initiativeness:** It is an inner urge in an individual to do or initiate something. Initiativeness means ability to lead from the front to achieve pre-determined realistic goals.
8. **Hard working:** It is an ability to work continuously and for sustained period of time without loosing head and heart despite of failure.

9. **Visualising:** It is an ability to foresight to predict the future business environment that likely to change in near future.
10. **Resourcefulness:** It means having all the necessary resources adequately for running the business entrepreneurs effectively and efficiently.
11. **Leadership:** It is an ability to lead the people in considerate and affective way. It involves getting positive feedback, initiate confidence, clarify the priorities, encourage for advancement, support to the employees etc.

3.8 Skills, Traits and Competencies of Successful Entrepreneurs

Entrepreneurial skills, traits and competencies are three different factors making entrepreneurs successful in true senses. Though their meaning is different they cannot consider isolated, as they act together. Their effectiveness while working depends upon each other.

Entrepreneurial skills are concerned with the ability of an entrepreneur to deal with different situations and in different social and economic forces. Skills refer to practical application of knowledge while working for attaining the goals of an organisation. It involves soft skills and hard skill. Both are equally important, especially from the view point of emerging entrepreneurs.

Entrepreneurial traits are judicious mixture of knowledge, skills and personal qualities. Traits are developed when these three attributes works together effectively. Further *entrepreneurial competencies* are concern with total productivity of an entrepreneur.It is the output of applications of skills and traits together. If the skills and traits work together effectively, the capacity to work i.e. productivity enhances positively and vice versa.

The list of skills, traits and competencies are inclusive and not exhaustive. Management thinkers are not unanimous on exhaustive list of and individual merit of skills, traits and competencies. Some of them are elaborated as under:

3.8.1. Communicating: Communicating is an ability to speak, write and listen clearly and effectively. Good and healthy communication provides the base for effective planning and organising, decision making, motivating, directing, relationship developing, seeking co-operation, and problem solving activities.

3.8.2. Decision Making: Decision making is an ability to take right decision at right time. Taking decision is a matter of specialised knowledge, experiences over the years and consultation with the experts. Taking wise decision at appropriate time is a master key of success.

3.8.3. Problem Solving: Problem solving is an ability to forecast the difficulties well in advance, assessing and analysing these scientifically finding the truth behind it and providing appropriate solution for removing those difficulties. Along with thorough knowledge and experiences, some time it requires laboratory work and experts guidance in this regard.

3.8.4. Motivating: Motivating is an ability to encourage the followers or the colleague in an organisation towards quality enhancement and goal achievement. It is the essence of eliciting positive response from internal and external stake holders, without hurting their feelings and self respect.

3.8.5. Visualising: Visualizing is an ability to predict future business environmental changes. It is again matter of business knowledge and experiences those alert against possible changes.

3.8.6. Relationship Developing: It is an ability to develop emotional stability among various internal and external stakeholders. Healthy relationship with employees motivates them to perform their jobs with high level of efficiency. With the help of good relations, customers are continued to patronize for longer period.

3.8.7. Opportunity Seeking: It is an ability to keep on searching chances of establishing new and profit making business organisations. Identifying and trapping an opportunity is a matter of knowledge, experiences, continuous observations and environmental changes.

3.8.8. Initiating: Initiation is an ability to lead from the front.It also refers as an inner urge to do something new and innovative activity for which he himself takes the lead to achieve his goal.

3.8.9. Risk Taking: Risk taking is an ability to assume calculated risk while planning and performing any business activity. Taking risk is a matter of experiences, knowledge and financial stability of an individual entrepreneur.

3.8.10. Planning and Organising: Planning is an ability to develop future course of action, keeping in mind the goals and objectives of an organisation to be achieved.Organising is the immediate step followed by planning in which necessary resources and factors of production are mobilised tactfully and systematically for further course of action.

3.8.11. Co-ordinating and Networking: Co-ordinating is an ability to see that all the activities are carried out by the colleague in different departments as per pre-determined plans in achieving the aims and objectives of business enterprise. It requires time setting, balancing and integrating diverse interest of various stakeholders.

Networking refers to the connecting all the persons and departments in an organisation with formal, clear effective communication system. Networking can be developed manually or with the help of information and communication technology.

3.8.12. Documenting and Presenting: Documenting is an ability to obtain, arrange, preserve and provide necessary documents for maintaining books of accounts and presenting as an evidence of particular transaction held in the past. Presenting is an ability to disclose or communicate necessary information orally or with the help of documents to make understand others.

3.8.13. Monitoring and Controlling: Monitoring is an ability to divert and control human resources recruited and engaged for specific purpose in achieving pre-determined aims and objectives of that business organisation in the best possible way. Controlling is an ability to guide the people and process of finding deviation between planned performance and actual performance and suggesting appropriate measures as and when needed.

3.8.14. Recruiting, Training and Mentoring: Recruiting is an ability of searching right manpower for right jobs, according to the needs and nature of job available. Providing training is an ability to impart basic knowledge about production, marketing etc. to build necessy skills, traits and competencies among persons engaged in particular table. Mentoring is an ability to develop the confidence and positive attitude among persons engaged in training for achieving personal and organisational aims and objectives.

3.8.15. Negotiating and Persuading: Negotiating is an ability to understand values, beliefs and thoughts associated with particular transaction and dealing with it successfully. Persuading is an ability to convince other through sound argument and logical reasoning for doing particular work in particular way required to perform.

3.8.16. Making Enterprises Successful: It is an ultimate ability of an entrepreneur to grab the success despite of any situation and any environmental condition. For making enterprises successful, requires strong desire of success, positive attitude and well directed motivation. It is also an ability to accept the challenges with great courage and positive inspiration in adverse socio-economic conditions.

3.9 Functions of Successful Entrepreneurs

Many thinkers believe that, the function of an entrepreneur begins with identification of an opportunity and ends with contribution towards nations' development. There are many functions expected to be performed by entrepreneurs which are elaborated as under.

3.9.1. Identification of an Opportunity: Identification of an opportunity involves investigating consumer's wants and needs, innovating something unconventional and useful, analysing the market potential and formulating strategy to face market conditions. It is an important and basic function of an entrepreneur, upon which future course of action is based.

3.9.2. Idea Generation: An idea generation is nothing but selection of product and production method. It requires clear vision and insight, perfect observation and experience, quality education and required training so as to bring idea into reality for precise idea generation.Entrepreneur should have thorough environmental study and deep market survey.

3.9.3. Assumption of Risk: Assumption of risk implies that taking moderate and bearable risk while conducting any business. In spite of thorough business knowledge and experiences over the years, an entrepreneur is expected to assume moderate risk while taking his decisions due to uncertain market conditions. Risk may be with regards to likes and dislikes of customers, investment of funds, adoption of technology, production method, marketing strategies, recruitment of staff, research activities etc. Greater the risk, larger the profit and vice versa.

3.9.4. Decision Making: An entrepreneur has to take many decisions frequently. Taking right decision, at right time is a master key to success. Taking decision is a matter of knowledge, skill, experience and financial position of that particular entrepreneur. Prospective changes may affect the decision. Decisions are to be taken to earn more profit as well as to minimise the losses in future.

3.9.5. Determination of Objectives: Every business activities always start with some basic objectives. An entrepreneur should know his aims and objective for which he conducts his business activities. Before starting any business activity, entrepreneur should clearly determine his objectives and then he should plan his further activities for achieving them systematically.

3.9.6. Raising of Funds: Raising necessary funds is the most important function of entrepreneur which he requires to perform very wisely and cautiously. For raising the funds economically, he should know the various sources of funds. He is expected to do a comparative study of these resources and then only appropriate source is to be selected. He should aware about the necessary documents and formalities to be fulfilled for this purpose.

3.9.7. Procurement of Immovable Assets: After raising necessary funds, an entrepreneur should procure immovable assets like land, factory building, machineries and equipments. Building is to be constructed and machineries are to be installed according to plan and under the guidance of experts.

3.9.8. Procurement of Movable Assets: For running enterprises smoothly and efficiently, entrepreneur requires to procure vehicles, raw material, oil and fuel, spares, equipments and tools, furniture, office equipments, stationery materials etc. These movable assets are required to purchase as per need and with minimum costs.

3.9.9. Recruitment of Manpower: This is an immensely important function of an entrepreneur. The success and the failure, especially in large scale organisation are mostly depending upon quality of manpower recruited, productivity and co-operation extended by them. While achieving the objectives of their business organisation in which they are working.

Recruitment of manpower involves estimating manpower, laying down of selection procedure, devising scheme of compensation and introducing rules and procedure for training and development of manpower.

3.9.10. Planning of Operational Activities: Before starting operational (Production etc.) activities an entrepreneur need them to plan well in advance in accordance with the aims and objectives of business organisation. Systematic plan of work avoids the wastage of time, money and energy. It also helps to improve quality of product to be produced in future.

3.9.11. Execution of Operational Activities: After framing the systematic plan of activities, entrepreneur needs to execute the same in pre-determined manner and within allotted time limit. Entrepreneur, of course requires to be flexible enough to cope with changing circumstances.

3.9.12. Employee Welfare: Employees are the true asset of any business organisation. Well disciplined, motivated, energetic employees with positive and innovative approaches help their employer for achieving great success. Therefore, taking care of employees is much important obligation of them.

Employee welfare involves paying salaries, wages, bonus etc. regularly, making provision for retirement benefits like pension, gratuity etc. providing non-monitory benefits like medicine, education, transportation, housing, and entertainment etc. facilities. Arranging workshops and training programmes regularly to enhance their existing skills, traits and competencies, are needed for better employee welfare.

3.9.13. Production and Market Research: Bearing innovative approaches and introducing innovations from time to time is an inherent characteristic of successful entrepreneur. For introducing innovations he should undertake research activities with regards to production, marketing etc. Application of new technology, motivation of employees, expansion of market, knowing consumers behaviour, enriching competitiveness only can be possible with undertaking research activities regularly.

3.9.14. Paying Revenues and Taxes: Entrepreneurs are expected to pay regularly and honestly revenues and taxes in accordance with the existing Acts and Laws to the Government and Local Bodies. It is their legal and moral obligation, they need to perform seriously.

3.9.15. Shouldering Corporate Social Responsibilities (CSR): Shouldering corporate social responsibility is a recent phenomena realised by the enterprises in all over the world. Entrepreneur as a owner of the business, cannot think only of his own benefit. Providing job opportunities to the people, conservation and preservation of natural resources, protecting environment from air, water and noise pollution, providing health, education, transport facilities etc. to the local people, developing healthy atmosphere are some of the assumed social responsibilities of today's entrepreneur.

3.9.16. Contributing Towards Nation's Development: One of the primary objectives of nation like India is to achieve balanced, rapid and sustained rate of economic development. It requires adequate amount of fertile land and other natural resources, skilled and motivated human resource, low cost and easily available capital and competent entrepreneurs who ultimately plans, organises, executes, directs, controls all the entrepreneurial activities for achieving success. Utilising all the scare resources optimally, producing quality products in the best interest of customers, paying taxes and revenues to the government regularly and honestly, creating job opportunities and wealth for the nation, contribute a lot for overall development of nation.

3.10 Conclusion

In a tradition oriented country like India, certain occupations are supposed to perform by the persons in specific castes and sub-castes. Business, trade and commercial activities are traditionally performed especially by upper caste people. Even today it is believed that entrepreneur are to be born and not made. New entrepreneurial culture and atmosphere, however proved this belief untrue. Now it is being proved that entrepreneurs not necessarily born in a family having business background and entrepreneurial culture. Many hardworking, self-confident, committed and visionary youths from non-business family background, especially from Scheduled Caste category have been emerged as successful entrepreneurs in business world. Their courage, confidence, work experience, motivational approaches and rare opportunities availed by them made it possible. Of course for creating energetic innovations and sharpening their existing skills, enlarging their traits and competencies target oriented Entrepreneurship Development Programme is desperately needed. As most of the SC entrepreneurs belongs to first generation entrepreneurs, Entrepreneurship Development Programme (EDP)is expected to play significant role in strengthening their entrepreneurial motivation and behaviour.

Reference

1. Vasant Desai, Small Scale Industries and Entrepreneurship, Himalaya Publishing House, 2010.
2. T. A. Kamble (2014), A Study of Entrepreneurship Development Among SC Category in Kolhapur District, Ph.D. Thesis submitted to Shivaji University, Kolhapur (India) pp. 81 to 86.
3. *Ibid.,* 181 to 182.

Chapter - IV

Measuring Entrepreneurship Development

4.1. Introduction

Entrepreneurship is one of the important means of socio-economic development of any country. The role of entrepreneur is not confined only to the establishment of enterprises but also includes creation of capacity to produce income, employment and wealth for the nation. These are the most significant indicators of economic development. Economic development is the ultimate outcome of entrepreneurial endeavours, in which entrepreneurs pool together and organises various factors of production, explore the opportunities, convert the ideas into viable business, produce the innovative goods and services and provide to the society people for satisfying their needs.

Entrepreneurship development has some elements of basic qualities, skills, traits and competencies possessed and cleverly used by an entrepreneur in his functioning. Entrepreneurship development is the indicator of financial stability as well as alertness towards ambitions and aspirations of particular entrepreneur. It is also associated with creation of goodwill, social status and development in researchable attitude. Entrepreneurship development therefore need to be assessed precisely and scientifically for further development in it.

4.2. Significance of Measuring Entrepreneurship Development

Measuring of Entrepreneurship Development of any respondent, involved in any economic activity is very much essential, as it shows the existing status of her or his development. It also shows proper direction needed for achieving overall entrepreneurial success in future. Measuring of entrepreneurship development is purely a matter of assessing the development of crucial factors involved in it. Many research studies in the past revels that the development of basic entrepreneurial qualities, skills, traits and competencies possessed by the entrepreneurs, development in their economic stability and the development in their alertness towards ambitions and aspirations are the major factor held responsible for entrepreneurship development in true sense. These deciding factors also comprises of some significant attributes which ultimately determines the level of entrepreneurial development of that particulars entrepreneur. These attributes need to be assessed individually and precisely.

4.3 Major Indicators and its Attributes

4.3.1. Entrepreneurial Qualities[1]: Entrepreneurial qualities are the essential, virtues or the characteristics of an entrepreneur; those are required for his or her overall entrepreneurial development. Some of the qualities are inherited from the descendent and many of them are obtained intentionally by hard work. It is proved that, an entrepreneur need not born, entrepreneur can be developed with his or her purposefully developed entrepreneurial qualities. Following are the major qualities required for entrepreneurship development.

4.3.1.1. Creativeness with Innovations: Creativeness is an ability to think and analyse the various problems in given situation and to create new things. Innovation is the spark of change that ignites improvement and progress in the state of things. It is the process of putting new, high values, ideas into action. Both the creativeness and innovations are two distinct concepts but should go hand in hand for the better results.

4.3.1.2. Visionary Approach: It is an ability of keen foresight to predict the future business environment, likely changes in market, customer's attitude, technological development, government policies etc.

4.3.1.3. Dynamism: It is an ability to create dynamic and energetic environment at work place. This positive and conducive atmosphere helps leader and his followers to act positively in achieving aims and objectives of an organisation within stipulated time and with lesser cost.

4.3.1.4. Self Confidence: It is a capacity to believe in own ability and strength, having full faith on own knowledge, skill and competencies.

4.3.1.5. Committment: It is an ability to fulfill own obligation by taking it as a moral binding irrespective of any sacrifice at any cost paid for.

4.3.2. Entrepreneurial Skills[2]: Skill refers to practical application of or use of knowledge. Skill is an ability to deal with situations, organisation and social, economic and technical forces as they suddenly emerged from time to time.

4.3.2.1. Planning and Organising: It is an ability to formulate realistic and achievable plans of future course of actions by keeping in mind the goals and objectives of an organisation and also to ensure proper execution of the same.

4.3.2.2. Motivating: Motivating refers to an ability to encourage the followers or the colleague in the organisation towards quality enhancement and goal achievements. It is an ability to elicit positive response from the colleague without hurting their fillings and self-respect.

4.3.2.3. Monitoring: It is an ability to ensure the performance of colleague or the subordinates that everything is carried out in the organisation as per the wishes of superiors or with the pre-determined rules and regulations, while achieving the goals in best possible manner.

4.3.2.4. Problem Solving: It is an ability to take problem as a challenge by putting best for finding out most appropriate solution for the same. It is also an ability to understand the problem and then evolve appropriate strategy to overcome the same.

4.3.2.5. Communicating: It is an ability to convey the message clearly and effectively.

4.3.3. Entrepreneurial Traits and Competencies[3]: Judicious mixture of entrepreneurial knowledge, skill and personal qualities are known as traits and competencies. An entrepreneur may possess certain traits and competencies and at the sometime it is possible to develop through training, experience and guidance.Following are the major traits and competencies required to be possessed by an entrepreneur.

4.3.3.1. Persuasiveness: It is a skill to convince and motivate others to do the work the way one want them to do, through his sound argument and logical reasoning. It is not physical but intellectual force on others to get perform pre-determined activity.

4.3.3.2. Initiativeness: It is an inner urge in an individual to do or initiate something. Initiativeness means ability to lead from the front to achieve the pre-determined realistic goals.

4.3.3.3. Risk Taking: It is an ability to take calculated risk in either while planning any major activity or while performing the same. It is not an attitude to depend upon chance factor to get expected results; instead it is an attempt to put an honest effort to get the desired result

4.3.3.4. Forecasting: Forecasting is the process of making predictions about general economic and market conditions as a basis for decision making by government and business.

4.3.3.5. Decision Making: It is an ability to take right decision at appropriate time by keeping in mind goals and objectives of an organisation and taking into consideration the strengths, weaknesses, opportunities and challenges before the organisation.

4.3.4. Entrepreneurial Ambitions and Aspirations[4]: High quality of ambitions and aspirations with consciousness is the essential characteristics of fully grown up entrepreneur. Strong ambitions and aspirations provide necessary energy to the entrepreneur for doing better and better. Following are the essential ambitions and aspiration to be developed.

4.3.4.1. Creating Wealth: It is expected that, an entrepreneur should possess high intensity of creating wealth for himself as well as for the nation. With the help of creativity, innovations, consistent hard-work, dynamism entrepreneur takes reasonable risk, hope for the better and perform his economic activity. Entrepreneurial development always helps for creating more and more wealth.

4.3.4.2. Generating Employment: It is expected that, by establishing enterprises, he should provide an employment opportunities to the job seekers. Ambition of generating employment opportunities for others is the sign of maturity of an entrepreneur.

4.3.4.3. Enhancing Standard of living: It is expected that, entrepreneur, by establishing enterprises, should create wealth, generate employment and income and enhance standard of living of himself and other people who are associated and engaged in performing economics activity along with him or her. Having strong wish of enhancing ones standard of living and working for other in this regard is the sign of ripeness in entrepreneurship.

4.3.4.4. Promoting National Interest: It is expected that, by establishing enterprises entrepreneur with his or her innovation and creativity, should produce huge amount of high quality products with minimum possible cost of production. Entrepreneur should always try to stimulate the progress by the means of his dynamic entrepreneurial qualities and should act as the pillar of economic development.

4.3.4.5. Leading the Industry: It is says that, an entrepreneur is fully grownup only when he or she is able to lead the people by fostering the confidence in them and motivating them for better performance consistently. As a leader, an entrepreneur should always look forward for the betterment of his enterprises and the betterment of whole industry in which he or she is engaged.

4.3.5. Entrepreneurial Economic Stability[5]: Economic stability through his or her enterprises is one of the prerequisite of entrepreneurial development. An entrepreneur is said to be developed only when he or she is completely economically stable. Following are the signals of complete economic stability.

4.3.5.1. Capacity to Invest Own Funds: It is assumed that successful and fully matured entrepreneur always possess the capacity of investing his or her own funds for more than 50% of total investment made in a particular business enterprise.

4.3.5.2. Capacity to Raise Borrowed Funds: It is assumed that successful and fully matured entrepreneur always possess the capacity of raising borrowed funds for more than 2.5 times than his or her own funds in a particular business enterprise.

4.3.5.3. Capacity to Repay Timely Borrowed Funds: It is assumed that successful and fully grown up entrepreneur always possess the capacity to repay timely his or her 100% borrowed funds well within the time which is invested in particular business enterprise.

4.3.5.4. Capacity to Earn Profit: It is assumed that the successful and fully grown up entrepreneur always possess the capacity of earning at least 15% profit on the total funds invested in a particular business enterprise.

4.3.5.5. Capacity to Reinvest Profit: It is assumed that successful and fully grown up entrepreneur always possess the capacity of reinvesting at least 25% total yearly profit earned in a particular business enterprise.

4.4. Assigning Values (Points) for each Indicator and its Attributes[6]:

Sr. No.	*Major Indicators*	*Maximum Scoring Points*	*Minimum Scoring Points (40% of Maximum Score)*
1.	Basic Qualities (5 Attributes x 4 Points)	20	8
2.	Skills (5 Attributes x 4 Points)	20	8
3.	Traits and Competencies (5 Attributes x 4 Points)	20	8
4.	Alertness towards Ambitions and Aspirations (5 Attributes x 4 Points)	20	8
5.	Economic stability (5 Attributes x 4 Points)	20	8
	Total	**100 Points**	**40 Points**

4.5 Calculation of Various Scores for Assessing Entrepreneurship Development

Sr. no	*Indicators and Attributes*	*For Individual Entrepreneur*				*#For Multiple Entrepreneurs. (for eg.100 Responded)*			
		*Actual Score	Value Assigned	Actual Total Score	Mini Score	Actual Score	Value Assigned	Actual Total Score	Mini. Score
I	**Basic Qualities**								
1.	Creativeness with Innovation	1	4	4		80	4	320	
2.	Visionary Approach	1	4	4		86	4	344	
3.	Dynamism	-	4	-		90	4	360	
4.	Self Confidence	1	4	4		95	4	380	
5.	Commitment	1	4	4		94	4	376	
	Total/ Average Total			**16**	**8**			**356**	**160**
II	**Skills**								
1.	Planning and Organizing	1	4	4		90	4	360	
2.	Motivating	1	4	4		80	4	320	
3.	Monitoring	-	4	-		80	4	320	
4.	Problem Solving	1	4	4		90	4	360	
5.	Communicating	1	4	4		90	4	360	
	Total / Average Total			**16**	**8**			**344**	**160**
III	**Traits and Competencies**								
1.	Persuasiveness	1	4	4		90	4	360	
2.	Risk Taking	1	4	4		90	4	360	
3.	Initiativeness	1	4	4		90	4	360	
4.	Forecasting	1	4	4		80	4	320	
5.	Decision Making	1	4	4		90	4	360	
	Total			**20**	**8**			**352**	**160**
IV	**Alertness to words Ambitions & Aspirations**								
1.	Creating Wealth	1	4	4		95	4	380	
2.	Generating Employment	1	4	4		90	4	360	
3.	Enhancing Standard of Living	1	4	4		95	4	380	
4.	Promoting National Intrest	1	4	4		95	4	380	
5.	Leading Industry	-	4	-		90	4	360	
	Total / Average Total			**16**	**8**			**372**	**160**
V	**Financial / Economic Stability**								
1.	Capacity to Invest own funds	-	4	-		80	4	320	
2.	Capacity to Raise Borrowed funds	1	4	4		80	4	320	
3.	Capacity to Repay Timely Borrowed Fund	1	4	4		80	4	320	
4.	Capacity to Earn Profit	1	4	4		100	4	400	
5.	Capacity to Reinvest profit	1	4	4		90	4	360	
	Total / Average Total			**16**	**8**			**344**	**160**

Note:

***1.** Actual score of individual entrepreneur as well as multiple entrepreneurs can be availed through the interview schedule.

#2. In case of Multiple Entrepreneurs, it is assumed that there are 100 entrepreneurs and figures shown their positive responses.

4.6. Assessing Entrepreneurship Development Index (EDI)[7]:

$$\text{Entrepreneurship Development Index (EDI)} = \frac{\text{Actual Score} - \text{Minimum Score}}{\text{Maximum Score} - \text{Minimum Score}}$$

4.6.1 EDI of Individual Entrepreneur

Here,		
	Actual Score for Indicator I =	16
	Actual Score for Indicator II =	16
	Actual Score for Indicator III =	20
	Actual Score for Indicator IV =	16
	Actual Score for Indicator V =	16
	Minimum Score for All Indicators =	8
	Maximum Score for All Indicators =	20

Therefore

(1) EDI for Indicator I = $\frac{16-8}{20-8} = \frac{8}{12} = 0.67$

(2) EDI for Indicator II = $\frac{16-8}{20-8} = \frac{8}{12} = 0.67$

(3) EDI for Indicator III = $\frac{20-8}{20-8} = \frac{12}{12} = 1$

(4) EDI for Indicator IV= $\frac{16-8}{20-8} = \frac{8}{12} = 0.67$

(5) EDI for Indicator V = $\frac{16-8}{20-8} = \frac{8}{12} = 0.67$

Final EDI $= \frac{0.67 + 0.67 + 1 + 0.67 + 0.67}{5}$

$= \frac{3.67}{5}$

$= 0.73$

4.6.2 : EDI of Multiple Entrepreneurs

Here, Actual Weighted Average Score for Indicator I = 356

Actual Weighted Average Score for Indicator II = 344

Actual Weighted Average Score for Indicator III = 352

Actual Weighted Average Score for Indicator IV = 372

Actual Weighted Average Score for Indicator V = 344

Maximum Weighted average Score for All Indicators = 400
(100 Respondents x 4 Points)

Minimum Weighted Average Score for All Indicators = 160
(40% of Maximum Score)

Therefore

(1) EDI for Indicator I = $\frac{356-160}{400-160} = \frac{196}{240} = 0.82$

(2) EDI for Indicator II = $\frac{344-160}{400-160} = \frac{184}{240} = 0.77$

(3) EDI for Indicator III = $\frac{352-160}{400-160} = \frac{192}{240} = 0.74$

(4) EDI for Indicator IV = $\frac{372-160}{400-160} = \frac{212}{240} = 0.88$

(5) EDI for Indicator V = $\frac{344-160}{400-160} = \frac{184}{240} = 0.77$

Final EDI = $\frac{0.82+0.77+0.74+0.88+0.77}{5}$

= $\frac{3.98}{5}$

= 0.80

4.7 Determination of Cut off Level to Assess Entrepreneurship Development

Level Of Growth	High Development	Medium Development	Low Development
Calculated EDI	0.80 and Above	0.60 to 0.80	Below 0.60

4.8 Determination of Level of Growth in Entrepreneurship Development[8]:

4.8.1. In Case of Individual Entrepreneur

As calculated EDI of individual = 0.73, which is between 0.60 to 0.80, growth in development will be treated as Medium Level Development.

4.8.2. In Case of Multiple Entrepreneurs

As calculated EDI of all the entrepreneurs= 0.80, which is between 0.60 to 0.80, growth in development will be treated as Medium Level Development.

4.9 Conclusion

India needs opportunity driven competent entrepreneurs rather than necessity driven or forced entrepreneurs. Such entrepreneurs would establish their enterprises, with aiming sustainable development. This requires inculcation and assessment of entrepreneurial values, skills, traits and competencies at their younger age. Entrepreneurship Development Index (EDI) certainly helps in assessing the level of their entrepreneurial development. It highlights strengths and weaknesses of particular entrepreneur. It indicates the possible opportunity of development in particular aspects. It also points out threatening areas those are needed to be considered seriously while in future development. Entrepreneurship Development Index (EDI) will serve as useful tool for precise and scientific assessment of growth of entrepreneurial development at individual as well as at collective level.

References

1. Vasant Desai, (2010), Small Scale Industries and Entrepreneurship Development, Himalaya Publishing House, pp. 419 to 427.
2. E. Gorden and K. Natrajan, (2009), Entrepreneurship Development, Himalaya Publishing House, pp. 16 to 18.
3. Ibid
4. Vasant Desai, (2010), Dynamics of Entrepreneurial Development and Management (Theory and Practice), Himalaya Publishing House, pp. 152 to 160.
5. Habibur Rehaman, AMH and Associates, (1979), Entrepreneurship and Small Enterprises Development in Bangladesh, Bureau of Business Research University of DACCA, Quoted by

S.G.Bhanushali, (2009), Entrepreneurial Development in Engg. Industry in Kolhapur District, a Ph.D. thesis submitted Shivaji University Kolhapur pp. 280.

6. Kamble T. A. (2014), A Study of Entrepreneurship Development among SC Category in Kolhapur District a Ph.D. thesis submitted Shivaji University Kolhapur pp. 193 to 194.
7. Dr Amartya Sen and Dr Sudhir Anand (1999), Quoted by S.K. Mishra and V. K. Puri (2005), Economic Development and Planning (Theory and Practice), Himalaya Publishing House, pp. 55 to 64.
8. Kamble T. A. (2014), A Study of Entrepreneurship Development among SC Category in Kolhapur District a Ph.D. thesis submitted Shivaji University Kolhapur pp. 193 to 194.

Chapter - V

SWOC Analysis of SC Entrepreneurs

6.1. Introduction

Every person has its own strength. He has its own weaknesses too. While developing the personality, everyone tries to enhance and develops its strengths and also tries to eliminate or minimizes its weaknesses. For overall development of personality, that person tries to search possible opportunities available for him and cleverly tries to repulses the challenges posed before him. History tells that many competent and accomplished persons, while developing themselves as successful entrepreneurs, they have analysed systematically and impartially their strengths and weaknesses in them. They fostered their inherent strengths diligencelly. They eliminated their weaknesses firmly and confidently. They have realised and created an opportunities before them and also repulses the challenges with strong determination and perseverance posed before them.

Few strengths are found in emerging entrepreneurs in SC category. There are some weaknesses in them too. These weaknesses are the result of their destitute socio-economic conditions in past. Inspite of this, they cannot afford to blem to such adverse socio-economic condition hence forth. The real question is that, how long and how many generations need to be destroyed ruthlessly on the background of their inhuman historical situation. Therefore wisely they must realise the opportunities available for them, especially in this globalised era. Rather, they should learn to create new opportunities for themselves and they must repulse the challenges before them firmly,then only new and emerging SC youth can survive in this global competition. In these days, strengths, weaknesses of SC entrepreneurs and opportunities as well as challenges before them can be analysed as below:

6.2. Strengths of SC Entrepreneurs

Entrepreneurs in Scheduled Castes category have their own and unique strong points. These are observed while studying their individual business profile and the style of conducting their business. Following are some of the major strong points strengthening SC entrepreneurs as successful entrepreneurs.

6.2.1. Strong Constitutional Provisions: Article 19 of the Constitution of India provides that, all the citizens of India, shall have right to practice any profession or to carry on any occupation, trade or business. This provision supports and motivates all SC people who have still engaged in their unhygienic, low paying and inhuman traditional occupation and divert towards new, innovative, high remunerative and respectful job opportunities for their overall development.

6.2.2. Tremendous Source of Inspiration: Majority of SC entrepreneursare originally inspired with the thoughts of their heros, the great social reformers like Rashirapita Jyotirao Phule, Chh. Shahu Raje, Dr Babasaheb Ambedkar etc. Thoughts and guidelines of these heros for changing socio-economic status are everything in the life of SC entrepreneurs. They are always ready to do anything to honour the precious thoughts wisely. This source of their inspiration is really tremendous.

6.2.3. Willingness for Occupational Mobility: History of SC entrepreneurs from which they emerged is worst. They were socially suppressed, economically exploited and politically neglected. Now they are realised about their unhygienic and low paying traditional occupations. They are strongly desired to divert towards innovative and modern occupations so as to improve their socio-economic status.

6.2.4. Hardworking Ability: Basically SC peoples are known for their honesty and hard working ability. It is one of the important qualities of successful entrepreneur. Their honesty and hardworking ability certainly help them for achieving entrepreneurial success.

6.2.5. Flexible Attitude: SC people and entrepreneurs among this category is found flexible and always ready to change themselves in accordance with changing circumstances. Flexibility in their attitude certainly helps them to accept the new challenges posed by environmental changes.

6.2.6. Commitment towards Obligations: SC entrepreneurs are basically known for their commitment towards their assigned duties. Strong commitment towards obligation in any business and fulfillment of them well within the time is dire need of success. SC entrepreneurs are found committed towards their entrepreneurial duties and achieve the success as they wish for changing their derogatory socio-economic status in Hindu social system.

6.2.7. Spread of Education: Now-a-day, all the SC people have realised the importance of education in their life. Strong inspiration from Dr Babasaheb Ambedkar for availing higher and specialised knowledge, have been proved master key in success. Constitutional provisions and Government efforts also causing spread of qualitative higher education among them. Educated SC youth are now trapping new and innovative business opportunities everywhere. Some of them are creating such opportunities with the help of quality knowledge they perceived.

6.2.8. Better Ethical Sense: Ethics is a broad concept which deals with moral principles or rules of conduct of human being at all level. It determines what is good and what is bad in the matter of moral duty and obligation of an individual or a group. It is well known fact that SC people, previously known as ex-untouchables were suppressed socially, exploited economically and were neglected politically at the hands of upper castes people in Hindu Social System. This background prevents them ethically from conducting unjustifiable and exploiting nature of behaves towards other person. Naturally by ethical, they inspire and motivate for performing their moral obligation with humanness. Many research studies have evident that the SC entrepreneurs wish to establish their entrepreneurial activities for providing employment opportunities for others and also for contributing towards nation's welfare.

6.2.9. Better Intiativeness: It is one of the important observations of the researchers that, SC entrepreneurs are comparatively better in taking intiativeness in their business. Initiativeness means an inner urge of an individual to do something different in better way. It is also an ability to lead from the front for achieving predetermined realistic goal. SC entrepreneurs have an ability to take the lead while doing any entrepreneurial work. They donot hesitate or come under pressure for such initiation. Of course effective and proper guidance as well as previous work experiences matters a lot for providing success to their initiativeness.

6.2.10. Assistance from Government: Since the independence Central and State Government have been providing economics and non-economic assistance to the SC entrepreneurs. They have been encouraging consistently for establishing micro and small entrepreneurs in rural, semi urban and in urban area throughout the country. Inclusive Policy of Government has been resulted fruitfully. Members of Dalit Indian Chember of Commerce in India (DICCI) are exhibiting their performance quite well due to such proactive approach and continuous encouragement of Central and State Government and its inclusive policy of economic development. Present Central Government also has been introduced schemes like "Funded to Non-funded", "Mudra Bank", "Jan Dhan Yojana" etc., those are supporting well to SC entrepreneurs. Such type of Government assistance and supportive atmosphere is strengthening them very well.

6.3. Weakness of SC entrepreneurs

Basically SC entrepreneur belongs to non-business family background. Most of them are the first learners as well as first generation entrepreneurs. Therefore inherently they are lacking basic entrepreneurial qualities and competencies in them. This adversity in them is emerged as their weaknesses. Following are some of the important weak points have been observed generally, while studying their business profile and style of managing their business affairs.

6.3.1. Associated with Traditional Occupations: Many SC entrepreneurs are associated with their traditional unhygienic, low skilled, low paying and mean work like leather tanning, shoe making, toilets and road cleaning, Some of them are engaged in making bamboo articles and making ropes of hemp etc. Many researchers found that especially in Chambhar and Dhor subcastes, people are engaged in their traditional jobs, those are laborious, unhealthy and derogatory to their life. SC entrepreneurs have not been diverted yet adequately towards new, innovative high paid and prestigious occupations.

6.3.2. Lack of Adequate Finance and Infrastructural Facilities: Basically SC entrepreneurs are known for their economic backwardness. They do not have inherited property or the strong sources of finance supporting them in their business activities. As they are lacking finance, they could not avail infrastructural facilities to run their business effectively. Due to economic backwardness, commercial banks and financial institutions also hesitate to provide required finance to them.

6.3.3. Lack of Courage and Fear of Failure: Many research studies have proved that SC entrepreneurs are lacking courage to initiate business activity by investing lakhs of rupees. They always seems fearful about their possible failure. Rather they think more about their failure, instead of their success. It may be because of their non-business family background and very little source of finance. They are also lacking risk bearing capacity which ultimately discourage them and force to think more on their failure.

6.3.4. Unfavourable Social Structure: Being SC entrepreneurs were previously known as untouchables in Hindu Social System, even today they are supposed to perform their traditional unhygienic and mean work as a part of their occupation. Even if any SC emerging youth tries to initiate new and innovative business activity, Hindu social system do not respond it positively.Upper castes people moves for undeclared boycott on the products of such SC entrepreneurs ruthlessly.

6.3.5. Lacking Researchable and Innovative Attitude: Many researchers have found that, SC entrepreneursare lacking researchable attitude in them. They donot think on innovative business activities too. Researchable attitude and innovative thinking requires,quality education and high achievement motivations. SC entrepreneurs donot provide adequate attention on required quality education either technical or non-technical. They are also lacking high achievement motivations in them.

6.3.6. Carelessness towards Changing Circumstances: A successful entrepreneur always aware about changing environmental circumstances. He takes his entrepreneurial decisions according to the changes in business environment. Financial, technological, marketing, etc. changes need to be adopted as and when required. SC entrepreneurs do not provide adequate attention on these changes. Their "Chalata Hai" attitude causing hurdles in achieving big success. They seems happy on the situation in which they are.

6.3.7. Technological Backwardness: Past research studies have proved that, SC entrepreneurs are technologically backward as compared to the entrepreneurs in other upper castes and religions. Their technological backwardness is the result of their low technical education, low investment capacity, carelessness towards changing technological atmosphere and lacking researchable attitude too. Their weakness in this important aspect make them difficult to survive in global competitions, as it hampers badly on their overall productivity.

6.3.8. Lacking Strong Motivations and Big Dreams: A successful entrepreneurs is always equipped with strong motivations. He loves to see big dreams. Motivation of achieving huge success and worldwide name as well as fame ignite a person internally to work hard consistently. SC entrepreneurs are found with poor motivations. They are lacking big dreams of achieving huge wealth and goodwill. They seems happy with moderate success. This causes hurdles in the way of their entrepreneurial development.

6.3.9. Lacking Risk Bearing Ability: Every entrepreneur is supposed to take moderate risk in his business activity. Greater the risk, greater the profit. Success of any business is dependingup on risk bearing ability of that owner of the business. SC entrepreneurs are lacking risk bearing ability. It is because majority of them are from poor families. Their economic resources are very weak. They cannot afford to lose what they have in their hand.

6.3.10. Lacking Effective Marketing Skill: Effective marketing skill is the master key for the success in any entrepreneurial activity. Producing good quality of product is not enough today. Attracting the consumers and satisfying them is very important. For effective marketing, branding the product, use of effective mode of advertisement, providing pre-sales and post sales services etc. is the real backbone of enhancing sale and profit.SC entrepreneurs have found very poor in these all aspects, which hampers badly on their success.

6.3.11. Poor Societal and Political Support: It is well known fact that, most of the SC entrepreneursare emerged from socially suppressed and economically exploited families. They are lacking strong economic and moral support in initiating and developing their enterprises. It is expected that society in general and Government in particular should provide helping hand by providing easy and adequate finance, higher and technical education, marketing assistance and even moral support too. Researchers in the past have found that the ultimate development of entrepreneur is largely depend upon societal and political support availed by him in his entrepreneurial activities. Unless SC entrepreneurs get strong support from society and Government, their success is like uphill task for them.

6.3.12. Unawareness of Government Assistance: Central Government and Sate Government too are providing economic and noneconomic support like entrepreneurial development training etc. to the emerging SC youths. Financial institutions like Mahatma Phule Backward Class Development Corporation are established. Many training centres are introduced for enhancing skills and competencies of SC entrepreneurs. However, it is the observation of many researchers that, majority of SC youth are not fully aware about these schemes and projects initiated for them. Therefore many of them could not benefited under these schemes in true sense.

6.4. Opportunities of SC Entrepreneurs

Though majority of SC entrepreneurs are belongs to non-business community, present free economy and globalisation atmosphere, have provided an ample opportunities for SC entrepreneurs. They only needed to be in search of business opportunities continuously and trapping the same at appropriate time. Following are some of the important opportunities available to them in this present global era.

6.4.1. Alertness toward Destitute Socio-Economic Situation: It is found through many research studies that, almost all the SC entrepreneurs are aware about their past destitute and degraded socio-economic history. They are also aware about their past derogatory social status. Now all of them desperately want to change this situation. With the help of entrepreneurship,they wish to come forward as good citizen of India and live with honour.

6.4.2. New Avenues through the Globalisation: Entrepreneursin SC category, of course those are educated and knowledgeable about globalisation, strongly believe that recent changes in worldwide economies have provided them new opportunities to start entrepreneurial activities. Especially, globalisation have widened the scope and the jurisdiction of their marketing. Now on this background of free economies there would be the lesser caste based restrictions on them.

6.4.3. Establishment of Special Training Schools and ITI Colleges: Government of India, State Governments and some Non-Government Agencies has been established special training schools and ITI colleges, in which adequate seats are reserved for SC trainees. It is good opportunityfor SC youths to sharpen their existing entrepreneurial skills and enhance the competencies in them. These institutes provides systematic practical training and entrepreneurial guidance especially in the field of management and marketing. This will help them to emerge as successful entrepreneur.

6.4.4. Bright Future for Agro Based Industries: Majority of SC entrepreneurs especially in rural area are belongs to agricultural background. Apart from their traditional caste based occupations; they use to go on field for their livelihood. They are aware about agriculture and agricultural process. SC youth from such a background have ample opportunities to initiate micro and small agricultural processing units in rural and semi-urban area. Governments also have been encouraging consistently for establishing and developing micro and small agro processing units. This entrepreneurial atmosphere is encouraging SC entrepreneurs to give up their traditional occupations and startup modern and agro based processing units in nearby villages.

6.4.5. An affirmative Action from Leading Entrepreneurs: The recent report of Confederation of Indian Industries (CII), has pointed out one very interesting fact that a company like Forbs Marshal Pvt. Ltd, Pune, is taking an Affirmative Action by supporting their trusted SC employees for establishing and running their business successfully. These SC employees are asked to provide qualitative raw material and spare parts for the company through their own units and thus regular market is assured for their products. Some time, economic and non-economic help is also provided to these ex-employees. Such a generous help and guidance in the form of 'Affirmative Action'from experienced business houses will certainly prove fruitful in an entrepreneurial development process of SC entrepreneurs.

6.4.6. Establishment of Self Help Group: Now-a-day's few SC entrepreneurs are being emerged and have started establishing as successful entrepreneurs. These numbers are need to be increased. There is bright scope on the background of recent positive business environmental changes to divert more SC youths towards entrepreneurial world. It is quite possible, if Self Help Groups are formed among existing SC entrepreneurs. Successful entrepreneurs will extend their every possible help to new and unexperienced entrepreneurs within their groups. They will be the guide, friends, philosophers and suppliers to each other.Their Self Help Groups will be the source of entrepreneurial movement in India.

6.4.7. Diluting Nature of Hindu Social System: It is now being observed that, previous traditional caste based Hindu social system especially in urban and semi-urban area is started diluting slowly. Upper castes people in Hindu religion are now accepting SC people as human being and also as an entrepreneurs. This is good and positive change which will certainly enhance the moral of new SC entrepreneurs.

6.4.8. Availability of Various Development Schemes: Especially after the independence, Central Government of India and even State Government have made available various entrepreneurial development schemes and programmes for encouraging micro and small SC entrepreneurs. Apart from providing formal training programmes, easy and adequate finance is being provided through the corporations like, Mahatma Phule Backward Class Development Corporation, Annabhau Sathe Vikas Maha Mandal, Leather Industries Development Corporation etc. Guidence in production and marketing activities is being provided to new and emerging SC entrepreneurs through the District Industries Centres. Technological and financial guidance is also being given to needy SC entrepreneurs under various schemes. This positive atmosphere provides good opportunity for grooming successful entrepreneurs from non-business community.

6.4.9. Diversion towards Non-Traditional and Profitable Occupation: Previously SC people were not allowed to choose any other fair and profit making occupation other than their traditional,unhygienic and low paying jobs. After the independence, constitutional provisions and inclusive policies of Government helped SC youths to divert towards non-traditional and profitable occupations. As said earlier, globalisation has made possible for SC entrepreneurs to choose any job and earn wealth as well as name and fame. Many avenues are opened up for SC youth where they can build their career. Many research studies have been proved that majority of SC youth have been diverted towards modern jobs due to positive business atmosphere in India.

6.4.10. Strong Motivation of Improvement in Socio-Economic Status: It is the finding of many socio-economic studies that, after 1980, SC entrepreneurs have been diverted themselves towards new and non-traditional occupations. Virtually, most of them are first generation entrepreneurs. Spread of education and economic motives have been playing positive role in changing their attitudes towards occupations. Their major sources of motivations are better dignity,better standard of living, self respect and also doing something meaningful which would generate employment for other too. Such type of positive motivation provides an opportunity for SC youth to come forward and initiate modern and highpaid economic activity.

6.5. Challenges before SC Entrepreneurs

There are certain challenges posed before SC entrepreneurs which are need to be accepted, if they want to survive and succeed in today's global competition. Many of challenges are posed as the result of their destitute socio economics condition and their non-business family background. Following are some of the important challenges, those are need to be accepted positively.

6.5.1. Slow Growth in Spread of Higher Education: Many research studies have found that, the spread of higher and technical education is the recent happening among SC people. This is the first generation of SC people taking higher and technical education required for business purpose. Naturally the growth in spread of higher education is very slow and limited to the urban setting only. Therefore entrepreneurial development among them is suffering a lot due to qualitative technical, managerial and business education. Improvement in the growth of higher education at this moment is the challenging task before poorly educated SC entrepreneurs.

6.5.2. Elimination of Socio-economic Discrimination: SC entrepreneurs are known as ex-untouchables. Previously they were exploited economically, suppressed socially and neglected politically, through the upper castes people in Hindu social system. Even today, especially in rural and semi-urban parts of India, this situation is not changed adequately, SC entrepreneurs are known by their castes and not by their entrepreneurial qualities.Despite of strong constitutional provisions and many Acts and Laws, elimination of socio-economic discrimination is not possible practically till today.Existence of casteism and socio-economic discrimination are pulling back to the SC entrepreneurs before they stabilise. Elimination of this kind of adverse conditions and making themselves comfortable is really challenging for them.

6.5.3. Breaching Social Barriers like Untouchability: Untouchability is the social practice in Hindu Social System, in which lower castes people are forbidden to be touched by the upper castes people. This practice is abolished constitutionally. It is not however abolished practically. Untouchability is observed even today especially in some rural and semi-urban parts of country and due to this observance, upper castes people hegitate to buy any product produced and sold by SC entrepreneurs. This practice limits the scope of entrepreneurial development in them. Observance of an intouchabilityis a crucial barrier in entrepreneurial development among SC people. Breaching this practice is the real challenge before SC entrepreneurs as well as it is challenge for Government also.

6.5.4. Facing Challenges posed by Globalisation: Many social scientists, researchers and entrepreneurs believe that, though the process of globalisation has opened up many avenues and widened the scope of entrepreneurial opportunities, they argues that globalisation has made an adverse impact on all social groups those have already been pushed down by centuries of oppression. They opioned that national policy supporting globalisation at one hand, ignoring the basic needs of poor Dalits, and compelling them,at other hand, to struggle for survive in ruthless global competition. Being SC entrepreneurs are very weak in mobilising and owning resources including economic and non-economic, there is very less chance for them to survive in tough global competition. Poor and resourceless SC entrepreneurs have to face new challenges posed by the globalisation process and to show their existence in global business.

6.5.5. Adopting New and Innovative Ways of Finance and Marketing: Recently it is observed that, majority of SC entrepreneurs have been diverting from their traditional occupations to new and innovative business activities. No doubt, these modern business activities help them to earn for their livelihood and to improve their social status. However the important thing is that, they are less aware in adopting new and innovative ways of raising finance as well as marketing their product. Basically they are economically poor. They have no enough property for offering security for loans to be raised from the banks and the financial institutions. Further banks donot provide them Letter of Credit, simply because they are wealthless. This limits in adopting new and better ways of finance.Further, SC entrepreneursare reluctant in adopting new and innovative ways of marketing too. It is mainly because of lack of adequate finance for advertisement etc. and lack of awareness about new marketing techniques. Their micro nature of business activities limits the scope of adopting new and innovative ways of finance and marketing. Thus it is challenge before them to adopt new, innovative and profitable ways of finance and marketing, so as to survive in global competition.

6.5.6 Developing Brand Name of Product: Successful entrepreneur always concentrate his attentionon developing his own brand name in the market. This help him to attract new customers as well as to confine old customers for his branded product. It is also required for better and effective advertisement. It creates the faith, affection and attachment about product in the mind of customer. Recent research studies have proved that, SC entrepreneurs with few exceptions are much careless in developing their own brand name and trade mark. Rather Majority of them are not aware about this important aspect of marketing at all. On the background of free economy, it is true challenge before SC entrepreneursto know the importance of branding and to learn for developing it for unlimited success.

6.5.7. Enhancing Quality Consciousness: It is observed through many research studies that SC entrepreneurs are less aware about maintaining quality of their product as compared to entrepreneurs in other sub-castes and religions. Their 'Chalata Hai'attitude about the quality of products shows sheer negligence in professional approach towards their business. In this competitive world, SC entrepreneurs should think seriously for enhancing their quality consciousness. It will improve their volume of sale and profit by improving trust worthiness among their customers. However, on the background of poor economic condition,poor technical know how and inadequate business knowledge,it seems uphill task for them.

6.5.8. Improving Researchable Attitude: Recent research studies have been witnessed that SC entrepreneurs are less prone towards researchable attitude which is infact the most important quality of successful business. This attitude helps to improve existing business atmosphere as well as it shows new and innovative ways of doing things in better ways. Researchable attitude helps to improve quality consciousness among entrepreneurs. Due to non-business family background, unsound financial position and lack of research based knowledge, improving their researchable ability is the challenging task for them.

6.5.9. Developing Visionary Approach: One of the most important quality needed for grabbing the entrepreneurial success is to have visionary approach in any businessman. It helps to predict the future business opportunities and makes alert towards possible risk in the business. Of course, it requires experience over the years and updated business knowledge. Forecasting the needs,wants and likings of customers, judging the technological changes, Government policies in future etc. helps in developing visionary approach of entrepreneurs. Majority of SC entrepreneurs are emerged from non-business family background, which eliminate the possibility of having vast business experiences. Therefore developing visionary approach on this background is challenging for un-experienced and first generation SC entrepreneurs.

6.5.10. Improving High Achievement Motivation: High achievement motivation is one of the most essential requirement for obtaining huge success. If the achievement motivations are poor, the level of success is also poor and vice versa. As the socio-economic history of SC entrepreneurs from where they have been brought up is generally destitute and unsound, they don't think more on high achievement with regards to wealth and goodwill. They just remain happy in improving existing conditions to some extent. Many of them seems happy on the situation in which they are at present. Making themselves hungry for more success on this background is really challenging one.

6.6. Suggestions for Various Stakeholders

Entrepreneurship development among SC people is a matter of nation's development. It is because, large portion of Indian SC population which is remained aloof from the process of economic development till today, could be diverted successfully towards way of progress, only if entrepreneurial development among them is made purposely. For this purpose various stakeholders like Central and State Government, Non Government Agencies, and society at large should extend their helping hand and positive co-operationto SC entrepreneurs. Further, SC entrepreneurs themselves are required to concentrate on certain issues while developing as successful entrepreneurs. Following are some important suggestions in this regard.

6.6.1. Suggestions for Government

6.6.1.1. Suggestions with Regards to Financial Assistance

1. Separate Nationalised Bank with at least Rs. 1000 crores of equity owned by Central Government should be established with its sizable amount of branches all over India to obtain required finance easily and without delay against the security of personal skill, experience and competencies instead of their tangible assets.
2. Existing Financial Institutions established for the support of SC Entrepreneurs may be converted into Development Banks for SC entrepreneurs with better plan, policies and goals.
3. Details of schemes related entrepreneurship development support meant for SCs, initiated by Central and State Governments should be mandatorily displayed, conveyed, monitored and deployed in each district with adequate transparency, to the SC people, in order to support and motivate them in their entrepreneurial development.
4. Funds should be earmarked, out of the total respective Entrepreneurship Development Plan, at least in proportion to the SC population of national, state and district level with separate budget head, non-divertible and non-lapsable status of funds.
5. Nationalised banks and public financial institutions should make compulsory to provide reservation in advancing loans at least in proportion to the SC entrepreneurs. There should be a separate and legally constituted mechanism to take periodical feedback and publish its report in nationwide news paper periodically.
6. Interest free loans up to Rs. 25 lakhs, should be provided to the educated, skilled and aspirant SC youths to initiate their entrepreneurial activities. Also proper and timely guidance to be provided with effective supervision on them.

7. All the nationalised banks, financial institutions, corporations and their loan distribution channel should be made user friendly and agent free. SC entrepreneurs should allow and encourage to have easy accessible interactions with responsible officers in the banks and corporations. Government should take adequate care to see that loan sanction and distribution is made corruption free.
8. SC entrepreneurs, those have taken loan from nationalised banks, financial institutions and corporations should be guided and encouraged for utilising those funds properly only for the purpose to which it was sanctioned. Also friendly mechanism should be developed to recover the loan on time, especially from profit making and well established entrepreneurs.
9. For effective utilisation of funds provided on the basis of subsidy, there is need to change approach from loosely targeted subsidies to creating and enabling environment. After examining physibility and viability of project, along with seed capital, support in the form of technical up gradation, market information, transport and communication services, insurance and warehousing facilities and such other support services of better quality with lowest cost should be provided.

6.6.1.2. Suggestions with Regards to Atmosphere and Accommodation

1. Government should initiate Plot Reservation Policy and adequate reservation of plots in every industrial estate areas should be provided for SC entrepreneurs for initiating their industrial activities and this reservation policy should be implemented strictly.
2. Proper motivation and preference should be given to SC entrepreneurs and promising candidates in quality Industrial Training Institutes to sharpen their skill and knowledge for making them capable entrepreneur.
3. Government should create conducive atmosphere which will ultimately helps in creating continuous flow of opportunity driven entrepreneurs especially in SC category, who in turn will create new and innovative enterprises, in the recent era of, globalised economy of this country.
4. Government should help (technical and infrastructural) in modernising the businesses belong to SCs to enable them to compete globally.

6.6.1.3. Suggestions with Regards to Training and Guidance

1. Spccial events like training programmes, workshops, seminars etc. are to be arranged frequently in collaboration with ITIs and local Universities, at district level as well as taluka levels for enhancing their skill competencies and their existing knowledge, with regards to production, marketing, finance, human resources development etc.
2. Entrepreneurship Development Programmes should be conducted seriously with planned syllabi and rigours training. Attempt should be made to develop soft skills as well as hard skills using advanced technology.

6.6.1.4. Suggestions with Regards to Marketing Support

1. SC entrepreneurs are to be motivated for quality production and opportunity should be given to export their products to overseas market along with their export credit and guarantee of collection of sales proceeds in abroad.
2. At every district level Common Trading Centre is to be established. Adequate spaces/ shops to be allotted to SC entrepreneurs for marketing their products.
3. Exhibition Centres cum Shopping Complexes should be constructed and allotted to the SC entrepreneurs for marketing their products especially in city area.
4. Encouragement should be given to SC entrepreneurs to form co-operative organisations or clusters of entrepreneurs so as to avail the benefit of good quality raw material, equipments and other supplies within time and reduced supply cost and also to help in marketing their products in collective form.
5. Considerable amount of tax relaxation especially in Goods and Service Tax (GST), Income Tax, Local Taxes etc. should be given for SC entrepreneurs at least for 10 years from the date of the establishment of particular enterprise.
6. As numbers of female entrepreneurs are very few,more encouragement should be given to female candidates those who are educated and willing to do any enterprising and self employed business activity, by providing them adequate finance, developing their skills and competencies and guiding them in production and marketing activities.

7. Adequate and timely guidance should be provided to SC entrepreneurs through separate mechanism for effective marketing of their products with prior declaration of Minimum Support Price.

6.6.2. Suggestions for Non-Government Organisations

1. Adequate efforts are needs to take in branding the products made by SC entrepreneurs. Government, NGOs, Universities, Marketing Federations, Chambers of Commerce should guide and help them in developing the brand of their products, this will help to promote their product in national as well as international market.
2. Most of the SC population is primarily depend on agriculture sector. Therefore surplus agriculture land and waste land too, may be distributed on priority basis, especially, to landless SC people for cultivation of agricultural raw material and establishment of business enterprises. NGOs must come forwards and support SC entrepreneurs in this regard.
3. Universities, ITIs and Management Institutes are suggested to play active result oriented role by frequently organising workshops and seminars at taluka places for aspirant SC youth for developing their skills, traits and competencies and also for inculcating business ethics and professionalism in them.

6.6.3 Suggestions for Society at Large.

1. Upper caste people in particular and society in general should give moral and psychological support to the SC entrepreneurs at their initial and development stage.
2. Upper caste people and social activist should help in maintaining healthy and conducive atmosphere without making any kind of discrimination towards SC entrepreneurs. Also they should help and encourage SC entrepreneurs for diverting SC entrepreneurs from traditional occupations to modern and innovating business.
3. Upper caste Hindu society should accept and recognise the existence of SC entrepreneurs, not by their nature of work they perform but by the business they run. Their recognition should be as an entrepreneur only.

6.6.4: Suggestions for SC Entrepreneurs

1. SC entrepreneurs should give up their "*Chalata hai*" attitude towards their business. They should be flexible enough to cope with changing business circumstances in this global era. Further, they should apply advanced production and marketing techniques to enhance quality of their product as well as to widen the jurisdiction of their marketing.
2. SC entrepreneurs should keep on updating their knowledge; skills traits as well as they should enhance their competencies with the help of formal training.
3. SC entrepreneur should utilise the amount of loan taken under various Government schemes, wisely and continuously to the purpose for which it was given. Also attempt should be made to repay the loan at their earliest.
4. SC entrepreneurs should adopt innovation in their products to attract new customers and to retain old customers. They also required adopting innovative approach of management to improve the quality of their functioning.
5. SC entrepreneurs should critically assess their strengths, weaknesses, opportunities as well as challenges before them. It is required for them to enhance their performance continuously.
6. Well established SC entrepreneur should extend their help and support to encourage the new, young and promising entrepreneurs. They should guide such young entrepreneur in finance, marketing, production, human resource development etc. aspects, by arranging regular meets and conferences.
7. SC entrepreneurs should adopt new and innovative advertisement means like television to advertise their products effectively and take them to national and international level. This will help them to retain their old customers as well as attract new customers in future.
8. SC entrepreneurs should take the information about existing schemes and programmes those are meant for their upliftment and should avail the benefits of it.
9. SC entrepreneurs should develop habit of maintaining regular books of accounts so as to record day-to-day's transactions and to find out financial result accurately at the end of their financial year.

10. SC entrepreneurs should seriously think on branding their products. This can be done with the help of NGOs like local Universities and Chamber of Commerce. This will help them marketing their products effectively.

6.7. Conclusion

Like entrepreneurs in any other sub-castes and religion, SC entrepreneurs have their own strengths and weakness. They have ample opportunities today, especially on the background of free economy and diluting nature social atmosphere to prove themselves as an able entrepreneur. Of course, on the background of their destitute socio-economic past history they have some unique challenges and threats before them. Previously SC sub-castes were known as non-business community and today, slowly but steadily they are diverting towards business community. It is true that, the social structure in which entrepreneurs were living and are being lived affects either positively or negatively on the behaviour of those entrepreneurs. It is also true that social structure, demand structure and opportunities structure limits the scope of entrepreneurial business. Despite all these social and economic barriers SC entrepreneurs are finding their space and position in entrepreneurial world.They are rightly proving that entrepreneurs are not born, they are made.

For greater success, SC entrepreneurs need to analysis scientifically their strengths and weaknesses. While adding strong points, they should try to minimise or eliminates totally if possible their weaknesses. They are advised to search more opportunities available for them for making themselves successful entrepreneurs. They should always alert while accepting challenges confidently. This is the rightway of their success. It is the duty of Government to provide appropriate atmosphere, where they can be grown up properly. Finally the society needs to extend its moral support and all possible help with proactive approach in this holy and national building process.

Annexure - I

List of Notified Scheduled Castes in India. The Scheduled Castes and Scheduled Tribes Order (Amendment) Act 1976

1. Ager
2. Anamuk
3. Aray Mala
4. Arwa Mala
5. Bahna, Bahana
6. Bakad, Bant
7. Balahi, Balai

*8. Basor, ***Burud***, Bansor, Bansodi

9. Beda Jangam, Bugda Jangam
10. Bedar

*11. Bhambi, Bhambhi, Asadaru, Asodi, Chamadia, Chamar, Chamari, ***Chambhar***, Chamgar, Haralayya, Harali, Khalpa, Machigar, Mochigar, Madar, Madig, Mochi, Telegu Mochi, Kamati Mochi, Ranigar Rohidas, Nona Ramnami, Rohit, Samgar, Samagara, Satnami, Surjyabanshi,Surjyaramnami

*12. ***Bhangi***, Mehtar, Olgana, Rukhi, Malkana, Halalkhor, Lalbegi, Balmiki, Korar, Zadmalli

13. Bindla
14. Byagara
15. Chalvadi, Channayya

16. Chenna Dasar, Holaya Dasar, Holeya Dasari
17. Dakkal, Dokkalwar
*18. ***Dhor***, Kakkayya, Kankkayya, Dohor
19. Dom, Dumar
20. Ellamalvar, Yellammalawandlu
21. Ganda, Gandi
22. Garoda, Garo
23. Ghasi, Ghasia
24. Halleer
25. Halsar, Haslar,Hulasvar, Halasvar.
26. Holar, Valhar.
27. Holaya, Holer, Holeya, Holiya.
28. Kaikadi, (in Akola, Amravati,Bhandara, Buldana, Nagpur, Wardha and Yavatmal Districts and Chandrapur District, other than Rajura tahsil)
29. Katia, Patharia,
30. Khangar, Kanera, Mirdha.
*31. ***Khatik***, Chikwa, Chikvi.
32. Kolupulvandlu.
33. Kori.
34. Lingader.
35. Madgi.
36. Madiga.
*37. ***Mahar,*** Mehra, Taral, Dhegu Megu.
38. Mahyavanshi, Dhed, Vankar, Maru Vankar.
39. Mala.
40. Mala Dasari.
41. Mala Hannai.
42. Mala Jangam.
43. Mala Masti.
44. Mala Sale, Netkani.
45. Mala Sanyasi.
*46. ***Mang***, Matang, Minimadig, Dankhni Mang, Mang Mahashi, Madari, Gaurdi, Radhe Mang.

47. Mang Garodi, Mang Garudi.
48. Manne.
49. Mashti.
50. Meghval, Menghvar.
51. Mitha Ayyalvar.
52. Mukri.
53. Nadia, Hadi.
54. Pasi.
55. Sansi.
56. Shenva,Chenva,Sedma,Ravat.
57. Sindholluu, Chindollu.
58. Tirgar,Tirbanda
59. Turi

*60. ***Neo Buddhists***

Annexure - II

Constitutional Provisions and Government Efforts for Well being of Scheduled Castes People in India

1. Constitutional Provisions

Article 14: Equality before law- The State shall not deny to any person equality before the law or the equal protection of the laws within the territory of India.

The doctrine of equality has many facets. It is a dynamic and an evolving concept. Equality of status and equality of opportunity is the main object of this article.

Article 15: Prohibition of discrimination on ground of religion, race, caste, sex or place of birth

1. The State shall not discriminate against any citizen on ground, only of religion, race, caste, sex, place of birth or any of them.
2. No citizen shall on grounds only of religion, race, caste, sex, place of birth or any of them, be subject to any disability, liability, restriction or condition with regards to -

   (a) Access to shop, public restaurants, hotels and places of public entertainment or

   (b) The use of well, tanks, bathing Ghats, roads and places of public resort, maintained wholly or partly out of State funds or dedicated to the use of general public.
3. Noting in this article or in clause (2) of article 29 shall prevent the State from making any special provision for the advancement of

any socially and educationally backward classes of citizen or for the Scheduled Castes and the Scheduled Tribes.

Article 16: Equality of Opportunity in Matters of Public Employment

1. There shall be equality of opportunity for all citizens in matters relating to employment or appointment to any office under the State.
2. No citizen shall, on grounds only of religion, race, caste, sex, place of birth or any of them be ineligible for, or discriminated against in respect of any employment or office under the State.
3. Nothing in this article shall prevent the State from making any provision for the reservation of appointments or posts in favours of any backward class of citizen which, in the opinion of State, is not adequately represented in the services under the State.

Article 17: Abolition of Untouchability

"Untouchability" is abolished and its practice in any form is forbidden. The enforcement of any disability arising out of "untouchability" shall be an offence punishable in accordance with the law.

Article 19: Right to Freedom of Occupation

1. All the citizens shall have right -
2. To practice any profession or to carry on any occupations trade or business.

Article 23: Right against Exploitation

1. Traffic in human being and 'beggar' and other similar forms of forced labour are prohibited and any contravention of this provision shall an offence punishable in accordance with law.
2. Nothing in this article shall prevent the State from imposing compulsory service for public purposes and in imposing such a service, State shall not make any discrimination on the grounds only of religion, race, caste or class or any of them.

Article 39: Certain Principles of Policy to be followed by the State

The State shall in particular direct its policy towards securing –

(a) That the citizen, men and women equally have a right to an adequate means of livelyhood.

(b) That the ownership and control of material resources of the community are so distributed as best to sub serve common good.

(c) That the operation of the economic system does not result in the concentration of wealth and means of production to the common detriment.

Article 46: Promotion of educational and economic interests of Scheduled castes, Scheduled Tribes and other weaker sections

The State shall promote with special care, the educational and economic interests of the weaker sections of the people, and in particular Scheduled Castes and Scheduled Tribes, and shall protect them from social injustice and all forms of exploitation.

Article 243D: Reservation of Seats

1. Seats shall be reserved for

a. Scheduled castes, in every Panchayat, and Article 243T – Reservation of seats for Scheduled Castes in every municipal corporation the number of seats so reserved shall bear, as nearly as may be the same portion of the total number of seats to be filled by direct election in that Panchayat, as the population of the Scheduled Castes in that Panchayat area, bears to the total population of that area, and such seats may be allotted by rotation to different constituencies in a Panchayat.

Article 330: Reservation of Seats for Scheduled Castes In The House of People-

1. Seats shall be reserved in the house of people for (a) the Scheduled Castes
2. The number of seats reserved in any State or Union Territory for the Scheduled Castes or the Scheduled Tribes under clause (1) shall bear, as nearly as may be, the same proportion to the total number of seats allotted to the State or union territory in the house of people in respect of which seats are so reserved bears to the total population of State or Union territory.

Article 332: Reservation of seats for Scheduled Caste In Legislative Assembly of every State

1. Seats shall be reserved for Scheduled Castes in the Legislative Assembly of every State.

2. The number of seats reserved for Scheduled Caste in Legislative Assembly of every State. Under clause (1) shall bear as nearly as may be, the same proportion to the total number of seats in the Assembly as the population of Scheduled Castes in the State.

Article 335: Claims of Scheduled Castes to services and posts

The claims of the members of Scheduled Castes shall be taken in to consideration consistently with the maintenance of the efficiency of administration in the making of appointments to services and posts to connection with the affairs of the Union or of a State.

Article 338: National Commission for the Scheduled Castes and Scheduled Tribes

There shall be a commission for the Scheduled Castes and Scheduled Tribes to be known as "The National Commission for the Scheduled Castes and Scheduled Tribes",

(1) It shall be duty of commission –

(a) To investigate and monitor all matters relating to the safeguard provided for the Scheduled Castes and Scheduled Tribes under this constitution or under any other law for the time being in force or under any order of the Government and to evaluate the working of such safeguard.

(b) To enquire into specific complaints with respect to the deprivation of right and safeguards of SC. and ST.

(c) To participate and advise on the planning process of socio-economic development of SC and ST and to evaluate the progress of their development under the Union and any State.

(d) To present to the President, annually and at such other times as the commission may deem fit, reports upon working of those safeguards.

(e) To discharge such other functions in relation to the protection, welfare and development and advancement of SC and ST as the president may subject to the provisions of any law made by parliament, by rule specify.

(f) The commission shall while investigating any matter referred to in sub-clause. (b) of clause (5), have all the powers of a Civil Court. Trying a suit and in particular in respect of the legal matters.

Article 340: Appointment of Commission to investigate the conditions of Backward Classes

1. The President may by order appoint a Commission consisting of such persons as he thinks fit to investigate the conditions of socially and economically backward classes within the territory of India, and the difficulties under which they labour and to make recommendations as to the steps that should be taken by the Union or any State to remove such difficulties and to improve their conditions as to the grants that should be made for the purpose by the Union or any State and the conditions subject to which such grants should be made, and the order appointing such commission shall define the procedure to be followed by the Commission.
2. A Commission so appointed shall investigate the matters referred to them and present to the president, a report setting out the facts as found by them and making such recommendations as they think proper.
3. The president shall cause a copy of the report so presented together with a memorandum explaining the action taken there on to be laid before each house of parliament.

Article 341: Scheduled Castes

1. The President may with respect to any State or Union Territory and where it is a State, after consultation with the Governor, thereof, by public notification, specify the castes, races or tribes or parts of or groups within castes, race or tribes which shall for the purpose of this constitution be deemed to be Scheduled Castes in relation to that State or Union territories as the case may be.
2. Parliament may by law included in or exclude from the list of Scheduled Castes specified in the notification issued under clause (1) any caste, race or tribe or part of or group within any caste race or tribe, but same as aforesaid, a notification, issued under the said clause shall not be varied by any subsequent notification.

Article 366: Definition of Scheduled Castes

(24) "Scheduled Castes" means such a caste, races or tribes or parts of or groups with in such castes, race or tribes as are deemed under Art-341 to be Scheduled Castes for the purpose of this constitution.

Reference: Constitution of India, Government of India, 1983.

Annexure - III

Major Scheduled Castes and their Traditional Occupations in Maharashtra and Kolhapur District

1. Mahar: Mahar caste people are found almost in every village in Maharashtra. The great thinkers like Mahatma Jyotiba Fule, Rajaram Shashtri Bhagawat, Dr Ketkar, S.M. Mate, V. R. Shinde, Dr John Wilson, Dr Haunton, Robertoson etc. strongly believes that, Maharas are the son of land of Maharashtra, and in ascent period, Maharashtra was the nation of Maharas. Even today Mahar people are numerically largest community among all the Scheduled Castes in Maharashtra.

According to Hindu caste system Maharas were the part of ***'Baluta'*** system. Their main duty was to undertake various tasks covered by the term ***Gavaki***. They were supposed to dispose of dead castle outside the village. Their duty was to guard village gates, to act as guide to the touring government officials, to make ***"Davandi"*** or the announcement of various religious functions throughout the village. As a part of their ***"Kotwalki"*** work they were entitled to guard village boundaries, to convey the message from government officials to villagers and vice versa. (Ref. - Bombay Gazetteer, 1931 Page - 82)

Even today some Mahar peoples are engaged in Gavaki and Balutedari work of their livelihood. They are serving their village people very honestly by disposing off dead cattles, sweeping village streets, cleaning the drainages, playing musical instruments and doing unhygienic labour work etc. Apart from this, some Mahar people are still working as ***bonded labours and vethbigars*** of their so-called Inamdar and Zamindar at their respective villages. Some are working as agriculture labours and marginal farmers. (Ref. Bombay Gazetteers, 1931, page. 112)

Now-a-days due to spread of education and the influencing thoughts of great social reformer Dr Babasaheb Ambedkar, Mahar peoples have been inspired a lot. They are taking higher education, migrating to cities and searching new and innovative occupations.

There are many sub-castes like ***Andman, Kabule, Kudwan, Gondwan, Ghadshi, Ghatkamali, Zade, Pan, Bele, Ladban, Sankamali, Saladi, Hedshi, Dhegu Megu, Somvanshi*** etc. are found in all parts of Maharashtra and Kolhapur district. (Maharashtra State Gazetteer, 1989, Page 164)

2. Chambhar: Chambhar or Charmkar castes community occupies third largest position among Scheduled Castes people in Maharashtra as well as in Kolhapur district. They claim descent from Aralaya, one of the son and worshiper of Lord Shiva's, who incurred Shiva displeasure by making pair of shoes of his own skin, which he presented to the Lord Shiva. As a punishment he was doomed to be a cobbler for life. As a class, Chambhars are quite honest hardworking and free from crime. This caste was treated as one of the twelve ***Balutedars***. Their major traditional occupation is tanning the leather, making shoe and chappals, making other leather articles like belt, purse etc. For this purpose, they use leather of cows, bullocks, buffalos, deers, sheeps, goats etc. Some people in this caste purchases hide from Mahar peoples and cure it themselves preparing foot wear and other leather articles.

Apart from those traditional occupations some people in this castes, are engaged in agriculture labour work and also working as marginal farmers. Few of them are engaged in selling readymade footwear through their shops in nearby markets. Some Ghatai workers, who seat and cobble at the road side, helps to shoe making cobblers with other people of their own castes.

Today Chambar castes peoples have benefitted to a considerable extent due to spread of education. Few of them are in high rank position in administrative and managerial level at various government and semi-government organisations.

Harale, Chiwale, Baite, Rohidasi, Aralayee etc. are some of the major sub-castes found in Kolhapur district. (Ref. Bombay Gazetteers,1931, page 110)

3. Mang: Mang or Matang castes occupies second rank in population and are found in almost all parts of Maharashtra and have been included in the category of Scheduled Castes. In the Hindu castes system Mang is an important Balutedar who serve daily village people and their local gods while performing religious functions, by playing musical instruments. Making ropes of hemp and selling them to local village farmers are important traditional occupations, usually they undertake for their livelihood. Apart from this Mang people especially in Kolhapur district, are engaged in making various bamboo and cane articles. They also make various kinds of brooms.

Mang people are music lovers. Especially at city level, they have their own Music Associations like ***Brass Band Company***. At the time of religious and cultural functions they play ***Sanai Choughada, Dhol-Tasha, Drums and Triple, Bagpipe etc.*** Some young people are also involved in ***Kalapathak and Tamasha*** Activities.

At present, as like people of Mahar and Chambhar community, Mang or Matang people are also have achieved their name and fame by adopting modern and profit making jobs and services and somehow they are trying to improve their standard of living and living with self esteem.

Mang, Mini-Madig, Mang-Garudi, Dakkhani Mang, Mang Mahashi, Madari, Radhe Mang etc. are some of the sub-castes found in Matang community in Maharashtra and in Kolhapur district. (Ref. Maharashtra State Gazetteer, 1989, p. 85)

4. Dhor: Dhor community has acquired its caste name from occupational association with "Dhor" Which means in Marathi ***"Cattle".*** This caste is found in southern part of Maharashtra and in and around Belgaum and Bijapur district of Karnataka State.

Dhor people were not treated as ***Balutedar,*** in the village level traditional supernumeracy claims.

Traditional occupations of Dhor people are to get the hide of dead castle from Mahar people and cure it on the bank of river or the stream nearby villages. Work of curing hide of dead animal and tanning the leather from it, takes about one month. It is very dirty, unhygienic and hard work causes skin diseases, Asthama, T.B. etc. serious illness to the workers.

Now-a-days the work of curing hide and tanning leather from it, is being done in the factories with greater efficiency and precautions, but still many people from Dhor community are engaged in this kind of dirty and unhygienic work for their livelyhood. (Ref. Maharashtra State Gazetteer, 1989, pages 56-57)

5. Bhangi: Bhangi peoples are also included in the schedule castes category. They are traditionally engaged in cleaning and scavenging public urines and toilets, especially in city area. They are known as night soil men. Most of the village Panchayats and Municipalities in Maharashtra and Kolhapur district have provided the jobs of sweeping public roads, flushing the gutters, removing Maila, or Malmutra outside the village and cities.

Bhangi peoples are found mostly in cities area. Even today most of the people from this community are engaged in this kind of dirty and unhygienic work, for their livelihood, and they earn negligible income from it. (Ref. Bombay State Gazetteer, 1931, page 109)

6. Burud: Burud people are found in Southern part of Maharashtra and especially in Kolhapur district, they believes that, due to their traditional occupations they are closely associated with Lord Shiva (Shankar) and his spouse Parvati. They were the part of Balutedari system and they were traditionally engaged in making various bamboo articles and cane articles like basket, grain, containers winnowing fans, birds cage, cane chairs, sofas, ladders, children cradles, mats, and various kinds of house hold articles.

The population of Burud community is considerable and found in rural and hilly areas, in all parts of Maharashtra and included in the list of Scheduled Caste after the independence. (Ref. Maharashtra State Gazetteer, 1989, pages 49,50)

7. Khatik: Khatik people in Maharashtra are few in numbers and they found rarely in Kolhapur district too. They are not considered as a part of Balutedari in Hindu social system. They are considered in the list of Scheduled Caste. Their traditional occupation is to cut the animals, especially sheep, and goats for the purpose of selling the meat. (Ref. Bombay Gazetteer, 1931, page 112)

8. Neo Buddhist: Neo Buddhist peoples are the followers of Lord Gautam Budha and his Dhamma. In post-independence period of India, socially suppressed and economically exploited ex-untouchables in Hindu religion, were woke up from their slavery and attracted towards new and innovative philosophy of life, giving top priority to *freedom, equality, brotherhood and non-violence.* Thanks to Dr Bhimarao alias Babasaheb Ambedkar for his pains taking and invaluable efforts in enlightening the spirit of humanity in the mind of those poor and uneducated people.

In the month of October of 1956, more than 3 Lakh people gave up their old and unwanted Hindu religion and accepted new identity as Budhist

(Followers of Gautam Budha) Those people, who were converted into Buddhist and also those are being converted so, are known as Neo Buddhist, and are included in the list of Scheduled Castes, for their social upliftment.

Neo Buddhists are well educated and civilised people. Though they are originally brought up from Hindu and other religions, they are now educating well, migrating towards cities and obtaining new and innovative job opportunities. They are few in numbers but more importantly they are mostly engaged in service sectors.

Annexure - IV

Dalit Indian Chamber of Commerce and Industries (DICCI)

Dr Babasaheb Ambedkar and his motivating thoughts are the real source of inspiration to all Scheduled Castes people in India. Entrepreneurs in various categories of Scheduled Castes are not exceptional to it. ***"Learn More, Come Together With Better Goal And Fight Against Unjustifiable Practices",*** was the revolutionary thought given by him. Keeping in mind his economic thoughts, "Scheduled Castes And Scheduled Tribes Chamber of Commerce " was established in 2003. The purpose of establishing SC and ST Chamber of Commerce was to push forward Scheduled Caste people and their ***Dalit movement*** in India, and also to give helping hand to the emerging entrepreneurs in this castes. However, within next two years, the working of SC and ST Chamber of Commerce was limiting the ambitions and aspirations of SC category and its entrepreneurs, ***"Dalit Indian Chamber of Commerce and Industries (DICCI)"*** established in the year 2005. The sole purpose of establishing DICCI was to strengthen and widen further the association of Indian Dalits and make it globalise in this new era.

Today, Dalit entrepreneurs, who are the honourable members of DICCI, are more than one lakh. Mr Milind Kamble, Chairman of DICCI and one of Dalit Crorepati in India, while sharing his experiences, Stated that, in India there are many of the areas which are not traditionally open to SC community. He further stated that the discrimination in India is not just on the ground of untouchability, it is also lies on opportunities, financial assistance and education. While opposing the State Policy, Mr Kamble argues that, why is it that State still indulge in skill development jargon for poor, and leadership development programme for rich? According to his

Profile of Top 20 Dalit Entrepreneurs Associated With DICCI In India

Sl. No.	*Name of the Entrepreneur*	*Status of the Entrepreneur*	*Annual Turnover Rs.*	*Family Background*
1.	Mr. Natha Ram	Chairman, Steelmont pvt. Ltd. Mumbai	600 crores	-----------------
2.	Mr. Ashok Khade	CEO, Das offshore, Engg. Ltd. Mumbai.	550 crores	A son of Cobbler from Sangli District, Brought up under staircase of Dockyard Mumbai First generation entrepreneur
3.	Miss. Kalpana Saroj	Chairperson, Kamani Tubes, Mumbai.	100 crores	First generation woman entrepreneur. Started Fashion Designing profession with loan of Rs. 40,000/-
4.	Mr. Milind Kamble	CME, Fortune Construction Co. ltd. Pune	101 crores	First generation entrepreneur, always dreaming for member of list of "Billionaire, published in Fortune Magazine
5.	Mr. Devajibhai Makwana	CEO, Suraj Filament, Bhavnagar Gujarath.	300 crores	----------------
6.	Mr. Sanjay Kshirsagar	M.D. Sound Concept, Mumbai	100 crores	First generation entrepreneur
7.	Mr. Swapnil Bhigardeve	M.D., Shree Khandoba Prasanna Sakhar Udyog, Pune	90 crores	First generation entrepreneur
8.	Mr. Milkiyat Chand	CEO, Jangal Exports, Ludhiyana.	70 crores	First generation entrepreneur, Started his career as Cutting Master
9.	Dr. Sushant Meshram	Owner, Multispeciality Hospital, Nagpur.	40 crores	First generation entrepreneur, son of Waiter, in Ordinance Factory, Pune
10.	Mr. Avinash Jagtap	C.M.D., Everest Spun Pipes, Pune	35 crores	-----------------
11.	Mr. Sushil Kumar	M.D., Simlex Engineers, Noida	25 crores	-----------------
12.	Mr. Mahavir Singh	M.D., Tricon Buildcon, Delhi	16 crores	-----------------
13.	Mr. Rajendra Gaikwad	M.D., GT Pest Control, Pune	15 crores	-----------------
14.	Mr. Dilip Bhai	CEO, Amba Synthetics, Bhavnagar, Gujarath.	15 crores	-----------------
15.	Mr. Pradip Nagrare	M.D., M/s P.K. Nagarare Const. Co., Nagpur	15 crores	-----------------
16.	Mr. Jitu Makwana	M.D. Millennium, Industries, Bhavnagar	10 crores	-----------------
17.	Mr. Sharath Babu	CEO, Food King, Chennai	10 crores	A son of Mother, selling Idalees for livelihood, grownup in slum area of Chennai, Studied in IIM and BITS
18.	Mr. Harsh Bhaskar	Director, Kota Tutorials, Agra	10 crores	-----------------
19.	Mr. Devanand	M.D., Payod Industries	7 crores	-----------------

Source – "Outlook", A Weekly News Magazine Vol. 17, Outlook Publishing India Pvt. Ltd. April 26 To May 2, 2011.

opinion, the belief of non-availability of caste based discrimination in corporate sectors in India, is purely misguiding and mistaken fact, rather corporate sector in India is also endowed with the lair of ancient ***Chaturvarna System.*** An attractive and invaluable proposal of any Dalit entrepreneur is thrown away into dust box, without verifying its viability and merits, as officials of high class society (so called savarn people) evaluate it from castism point of view.

Mr Mukul Wasnik, Hon'ble Union Minister of Human Welfare and Social Justices, admitted that apart from education and technical assistance to SCs and STs, government is looking forward to bring others policies like leadership development for emerging entrepreneurs in particular castes.

Annexure-V

List of New and Innovative, Tiny and Small Non-Traditional Occupations Available for SC Entrepreneurs

1. Food Processing Business

1. Bakery Production,
2. Hotel and Catering Management
3. Grapes Processing and Wine Products
4. Cashew Nut Processing
5. Fruits and Vegetable Processing
6. Milk Processing

2. Agro Based Business

1. Sheeps, Goats, Emmus and Rabit Farming
2. Cows and Buffalo Farming,
3. Producing Food Grains, Fruits and Vegetables,
4. Food Processing Business,
5. Cultivation of Medicinal Plants,
6. Green Houses and Flowery Culture,
7. Vermi Compost and Organic Fertilisers,
8. Plantation and Tissue Culture Management,
9. Sericulture and Pessiculture,
10. Honeybee Farming,
11. Fisheries In Sweet Water.

3. Construction Business

1. Residential and Commercial Houses Developers
2. Architecturing.
3. Interior Designing
4. Construction of Roads, Dams, Bridges etc.
5. Massionary Work, Centering, Plumbing, Electrification, Painting, Fabricating,
6. Floor Fitting Contractors.

4. Electricals and Electronics

1. Non Conventional/ Non-Traditional Energy Production
2. Production of Electrical And Electronics Goods
3. Repairs of Electrical And Electronics Appliances
4. Trading of Electronics And Electrical Goods

5. Service Sector

1. Accounting and Auditing
2. Tax Consulting
3. Judges, Advocates And Consultants
4. Doctors and Medical Practitioners
5. Engineers and Architects.
6. Teachers and Professors.
7. Motor And Vehicle Repairing
8. Hair Cutting And Saloon
9. Tailoring And Fashion Designing
10. Social Worker and Councilor

6. Artisan

1. Making Articles from Bamboo and Wet Sticks.
2. Making Wooden Toys.
3. Production of Agarbattis and Candles.
4. Shoe Making.
5. Making Wooden Furniture/ Carpentry Work.
6. Clay Articles Making.
7. Stone and Magnetic Production.
8. Handlooms and Embroidery Work.

7. Health and Hygiene

1. Panchkarma
2. Beauty Parlour and Masaj Centre
3. Health Consultants
4. Diet Consultants

Annexure-VI

Some Key Parameters of Enterprises in Indian Scenario

Sr. No.	*Parameters*	*Tiny Enterprises*	*Small Enterprises*	*Medium Enterprises*	*Large Enterprises*
1.	Investment in Plant and Machinery	Up to 25 lakhs	Upto Rs. 100 lakhs to 300 lakhs	Upto Rs. 5 crores	Above Rs. 5 crore
2.	Employment	Less than 5 persons	Less than 100 persons	Less than 200 persons	Above 200 persons
3.	Production	Tiny	Small	Medium	Large
4.	Technology	NIL	Low medium	High	High
5.	Brands	NIL	Rarely and Few	Fair	Good
6.	Organization	Proprietary	Proprietary and Partnership	Partnership and Pvt. Ltd. Co.	Public Ltd. Co.
7.	Management	Direct	Direct	Professional	Professional and Organized
8.	Gestation (Period)	NIL	Short	Medium	Long
9.	H.R.D.	NIL	NIL	Fair	Good
10.	Profit	Low	Good	V. Good	Huge.

Ref. – Dr Vasant Desai, Small Scale Industries and Entrepreneurship, Himalaya Publishing House. Page No. X, Section - I

Bibliography

01. Alexander K.C., (July 1988), Changing Status of Pulayas, Harijan of Kerala, Economic and Political Weekly, Page 321. Quoted by S.M. Dahiwale in Emerging Entrepreneurship among Scheduled Castes.

02. Ambedkar's B.R., Writing and Speeches (1989), Vol. 5, Government of Maharashtra.

03. Ambedkar B.R., (1989), Rock on Which Hindu Have Built Their Houses, Dr Babasaheb Ambedkar's Writing and Speeches, Vol. 7 Government of Maharashtra.

04. Barna J. J., (1960), Industrial Entrepreneurship in Madras States, Asia Publishing House Bombay.

05. Bendix and Lipset (Ed), (1966), Class, Status and Power, Free Press Journal, pp. 591 To 601 quoted by S. M. Dahiwale in Emerging Entrepreneurship Among Scheduled Castes.

06. Bhanushali S. G., (2009), Entrepreneurial Development in Engg. Industry in Kolhapur City. Ph.D Thesis submitted to Shivaji University, Kolhapur.

07. Bhatia B.S., (1974), New Industrial Entrepreneurs, Their Origin and Problems, Journal of General Management. Vol. 2, pp. 69 To 79.

08. Bharatiya Shishu Evom Mahila Vividh Vikas Samiti, (2009-10), New Delhi, Researcher Study on Entrepreneurial Challenges for SC Persons in India Sponsored and Funded By Planning Commission Government of India New Delhi, pp. 18 to 70.

09. Bose N. K., (1976), The Structure of Hindu Society, (Trans) Sangam Books, p. 51 quoted by S. M. Dahiwale in Emerging Entrepreneurship Among Scheduled Castes.

10. Burate Prakash Yashwant, (March 2008), Views of Dr Babasaheb Ambedkar on Social Exclusion and Inclusive Policy Social Exclusions and Inclusive Policies In South Asia At Shivaji University, Kolhapur.

11. B. Rajsekaran, (4 Dec 2003), Entrepreneurial Performance SEDEME Vol. 30, pp. 10 to 13.
12. Census of India, (2011), Government of India.
13. Chandrapal, (2010) (Adviser, Planning, Commission, Government of India, New Delhi) Action Point for Development of Schedule Castes and Schedule Tribes pp. 9 to 15.
14. CII, (2011), A Report on Affirmative Action, With Reference to Forbs Marshell Pvt. Ltd.: A Case Study.
15. Dahiwale S. M., (1989), Emerging Entrepreneurship among Scheduled Castes, Research Thesis submitted to Shivaji University Kolhapur.
16. Desai Vasant, (2010), Dynamics of Entrepreneurial Development and Management (Theory and Practice), Himalaya Publishing House, pp. 152 to 160.
17. Desai Vasant, (2010), Small Scale Industries and Entrepreneurship, Himalaya Publishing House.
18. Deshpande M. U., (1964), Entrepreneurship of Small Scale Industries, Deep and Deep Publication, New Delhi, p. 282.
19. Deshmukh Prabhakar, (June 2002), Udyojakata Vikas: Sankalpana Ani Vyavhar, Pimpalapure and Co. Nagpur, pp. 216 to 245.
20. Devis Kith and Blomstrom, (1971), Business Society and Environment, McGraw Hill, New York, p. 11.
21. Doshi Harish, (1980), Occupational Diversification and Removal of Untouchability, Gujarat University, Ahamdabad.
22. D. Narendra Kumar, (1995), Entrepreneurship in Small Scale Sector, Discovery Publishing House, New Delhi, pp. 150 To 161.
23. Ernest Krausz, (1972), Factors of Social Mobility in British Minority Groups, The British Journal of Sociology Vol. 23, pp. 272 to 283 quoted by S.M. Dahiwale in Emerging Entrepreneurship Among Scheduled Castes.
24. E. Gorden and K. Natrajan, (2009), Entrepreneurship Development, Himalaya Publishing House, pp. 16 to 18.
25. Fox R.G., (1969), From Zamindar to Ballot Box, Cornell University Press, New York.
26. Gangrde K.D., (1975), Social Mobility in India, a Study of Depressed Class, Man in India, Vol. No.53, Sept. p. 252.
27. Gare Govind and Limaye Shirubhau, (1970), Maharashtratil Dalit – Shodh Anni Bodh" (Marathi), Sahadhya Prakashan, Mumbai, pp. 68 to 166.

28. Ghurye G.S., (1978), Caste, Class and Occupation, Popular Book Depot. Mumbai. p. 142, quoted by V. N. Gajendragadkar, Castes, Races in India.
29. Guha Almendu, (29th Aug. 1970), Parasi Seths and Entrepreneurs, Economic and Political Weekly Vol. V, p. 35.
30. Habibur Rehaman, AMH and Associates, (1979), Entrepreneurship and Small Enterprises Development in Bangladesh, Bureau of Business Research University of DACCA, Quoted by S.G.Bhanushali, (2009), Entrepreneurial Development in Engg. Industry in Kolhapur District, a Ph.D. thesis submitted Shivaji University Kolhapur pp. 280.
31. Haris F. R., (1925) J.N.Tata: A Chronicle of His Life", Oxford University Press, London.
32. Ito Shoji, (Sept 1966), A Note on Business Combine In India, Special Reference to Nathi Kotti Chettaiare, In Developing Economy, Vol. IV, 3, pp. 367 To 380.
33. Iyaer Lakshmi, khanna Tarun, Varshney Asutosh, (Feb 9, 2013), Caste and Entrepreneurship in India; Economic and Political Weekly, Vol. XLVII, pp. 52 to 59.
34. Jackson F.E., Fox W.S. and Croulett Jr., (1970), Religion and Occupational Achievement, American Sociological Review, Vol. 35, pp. 51 To 60.
35. Javillonar G. V. and Peter G. R., (1987), Sociological and Psychological Aspects of Indian Entrepreneurship, The British Journal of Sociology Vol. 24, PP 314-328.
36. Jodhaka Surindar S., (Nov. 2010), Dalits In Business; Self Employed Scheduled Castes in North-west India, Working Paper Series Vol. IV, By Indian Institute of Dalit Studies.
37. Jogdand P.G., (March 2008), Understanding Social Exclusion and Discrimination: A Sociological Perspective, A Seminar Paper Presented at International Seminar on Social Exclusion and Inclusive Policies in South Asia. Organised by Shivaji University Kolhapur.
38. Joshi N.V., (Ed), (2001), Ravindra Thakur, Pune Varnan, Mudra Prakashan, Kolhapur, p. 61.
39. Kamble T. A., (2014), A Study of Entrepreneurship Development among SC Category in Kolhapur District a Ph.D. thesis submitted by Shivaji University Kolhapur pp. 193 to 194.
40. Kamble B. N., (1995), Effectiveness of Developmental Programmes for SC and ST In Maharashtra. A Ph.D. thesis, submitted to Pune University.

41. Kapase G. P., (2003), An analytical study of Woman Entrepreneurship in Marathwada Ph.D. thesis submitted to Shivaji University, Kolhapur.

42. Kalam Singh, (1984), Occupational Mobility in Rural Setting, The Indian Journal of Social Research, Vol. 25.

43. Kelly Jonathan, (March 1978), Wealth and Family Background in the Occupational Career, The British Journal of Sociology, Vol. 29, pp. 98 to 106 quoted by S.M. Dahiwale in Emerging Entrepreneurship Among Scheduled Castes.

44. Khan Mumtaz Ali, (1980), Scheduled Castes and Their Status in India, Uppal Publication House, New Dehli, pp. 127 to 128.

45. Kharat Shankarrao, (Ed.) (2006), Dr Babsaheb Ambedkar Yanchi Atmakatha, Indrayani Sahitya Prakashan, pp. 40-41.

46. Kotwal K.M., (Dec.2004), Role of MCED and DIC in Entrepreneurship Development, In Sindhudurg District. M. Phil Dissertation submitted to Shivaji University, Kolhapur.

47. Kharat Shankarrao, (2006), Samajik Chalvalicha Itihas, Indrayani Prakashan, Pune, retrieved from Saint Eknath, Eknathi Bhagwat. Shlok 17 to 19, pp. 697 to 701. Adhyay 17-82, 17-83, pp. 693 to 702.

48. Kirtiraj D.C., (October 2007), Study of Impact of Globalisation on Socio-economic status of Neo-Buddhist Community in Akola District., Ph.D. thesis submitted to Pune University.

49. Kumar Raj, (2000), Article on Globalisation and Dalit Culture, P.G. Jogdand (ed). pp. 89-90.

50. Kunkel John, (1970), Society and Economic Growth: A Behavioural Perspective of Social Changes, Oxford University Press London, pp. 260-270, quoted by Dr Prabhakar Deshmukh, Udyojakta Vikas Pipalapure Prakashan Nagpur, 2002.

51. Kulkarni M.G., and Hiramani A.B., (Sept. 1975) Occupational Pattern, In Two Marathwada Villages; A Comparative Study, University Journal Vol. – XIV, Page 93 To 97.

52. Kurane Anjali, (April 1997), Ethnic Identity and Social Mobility; A Case study of Buddhists in Pune, Ph. D Thesis Submitted to Pune University,

53. K. Ravi Chandra, (1978), An Entrepreneurial Success; A Psychological Study, in Hyderabad City of Andhra Pradesh.

54. Liberson S., and Fuguilt G.V., (September 1967), Negro- White Occupational Differences in the Absence of Discrimination, American

Journal of Sociology, Vol. 73, No. 2, pp. 197 and 198 quoted by S.M. Dahiwale in Emerging Entrepreneurship Among Scheduled Castes.

55 Mac Crory J. T., (1956), Small Industrialists in North Indian Towns. A Case Study in Latest Industrial Potential, Ministry of Commerce and Industries, Government of India.

56. Mac Clelland David D., (1961), The Achieving Society, The Free Press Journal, New York.

57. Mahind B.S., (2008), A Study of Entrepreneurship Development In Khanapur, Vita Towns In Sangli District. Ph.D thesis submitted to Shivaji University, Kolhapur.

58. Mehara Savita (et al), (1984), Changing Correspondence between Castes and Occupation; A Socio-Economic Analysis, The Eastern Anthropologist Vol. 37, p. 335.

59. Milman H. A., (1954), The Marwadi; A Study of Group of Trading Castes, Unpublished M.A. Thesis of University of California, Berkeley.

60. M. Kasi Reddy, (Jan-Mar 2003), Entrepreneurial Process among SCs and STs in Andhra Pradesh, The Indian Journal of Commerce Vol. 56, pp. 83 To 87.

61. Nafzigar E.W., (Jan 1975), Class, Caste and Community of South India Industrialist; An Examination of Horatio Alger Model In The Journal Of Development Studies Vol. II, No.2, , pp. 131 To 148.

62. Pandit D. P., (1995), Creative Response in Indian Economy; A Regional Analysis, The Economic and Political Weekly, Vol. IX No. 8 and 9, pp. 283 to 286 and 315 to 317.

63. Pathak H. N., (Nov. 1972), The Entrepreneurs Technician and Managers, In Small Scale Units, Economic and Political Weekly, Review of Management Vol. VII, pp. 179- 187.

64. Patankar Bharat, (2000), New Economic Policy and Dalit: Alternatives of Development, P.G. Jogdand (ed) pp. 58 to 67.

65. Patwardhan Sunanda, (1973), Changes among India's Harijans, Orient Longman Publications, Page 203.

66. Patwardhan Sunanda, (1965), A Study of Scheduled Castes in an Urban Setting, A Ph.D. thesis, submitted to Pune University.

67. Planning Commission of India, New Delhi (2006), General Guidelines for Formulation, Implementation and Monitoring of Schedule Caste Sub Plan (SCSP) For States and Central Ministry Department, pp. 9 to 15.

68. P. Ramkrishnan, (July 1971), New Entrepreneurship in Small Scale Industries in New Delhi, Economics and Scientific Research Foundation, New Delhi, p. 27.
69. Rahate J. V., (1985), Modernisation among Scheduled Caste, With Special Reference to Maharas, Weavers and Sweepers of Nagpur City; Ph.D. Thesis submitted to Marathwada University Aurangabad, pp. 188 to 198.
70. Ransford Edward H., and Jeffries Vincent, (1980), Social Stratification – A Multiple Hierarchy Approach, Allyn Bacon, pp. 156 to 174 quoted by S.M. Dahiwale in Emerging Entrepreneurship Among Scheduled Castes.
71. R. Madhavan, (Jan 28 to Feb 4), Pattern of Enterprises of Chattiare, In Malaya, 1880 To 1930, Economic and Political Weekly Vol. 13 No 4-5, , pp. 146 To 154.
72. R. Owen, (1982), Peasant Entrepreneurs in Industrial City in Singer M (Ed), pp. 133 to 166.
73. Saini J.S., (1997), Entrepreneurship Development Programmes and its Practices, Deep and Deep Publications, New Delhi, pp. 200-339.
74. Salunkhe P.B., Mali M.G., (Ed.), (1994), Chh. Shahu; The Pillar of Social Democracy, Education Dept. Government of Maharashtra, pp. 28 to 45.
75. Sarkar R.M., (2006), Dalits in India – Past and Present, Serial Publications Delhi (ed).
76. Sarwate Dilip M., (1988), Entrepreneurial Development: Concept and Practices, Everest Publishing House, Pune, p. 67.
77. Sen Amartya and Anand Sudhir, (1999), Quoted by S.K. Mishra and V. K. Puri (2005), Economic Development and Planning (Theory and Practice), Himalaya Publishing House, pp. 55 to 64.
78. Sharma Govind, (1984), Trends in the Study of Scheduled Castes, The Journal of Indian Anthropological Asso. New Delhi, Vol. 14, p. 119.
79. Sharma K. L., (1975), Entrepreneurial Performance in Role Perspective, Abhinav Publication, New Delhi.
80. Sharma R.A. (1980), Entrepreneurial Changes is Indian Industries, Sterling Publishers, New Delhi.
81. Sharma S. P., (Dec.1965), Emergence of Industrial Entrepreneur: A Sociological Process, In Indian Journal of Commerce, Vol. xiii, Part iv, N.65, pp. 369-373.

82. Shastri Uttara, (1998), Neo Buddhists: As Marginal Group in India, – Ph.D. thesis Submitted to Pune University.
83. Shinde D. D., (2002), Role of Mahatma Phule Backward Class Development Corporation, In Economic Upliftment of SC Community, A Case Study of Kolhapur City. M. Phil Dissertation submitted to Shivaji University, Kolhapur.
84. Suri R. K. and Sharma, (2007), Entrepreneurship Development, Kitab Mahal Publications, pp. 301 to 315.
85. S. Ananth, T. Sabri OnCu, (Feb. 16, 2013), Challenges to Financial Inclusion in India, The case study of Andhra pradesh, Economic and Political Weekly, Vol. XLVIII, p. 77.
86. S. Ashok Kumar, (1974), Entrepreneurship in Small Industry, Discovery Publishing House, New Delhi. p. 43.
87. Thorat Sukhdeo, (May 2005), Why Reservation in Private Sector is Necessary, A Seminar Paper Presented in the International Conference, Hydrabad, pp. 30-35.
88. Thorat S.K., (2002), Ambedkar's Economic Ideas and Liberalisation: Emerging Challenges before Dalit. 100 years of Reservation, An Appraisal and Assessment, Under the Ages of Republican Party of India, Hyderabad (AP).
89. Treiman, Donald J and Terrel Kermit, (1975), The Process of Status Attainment in the United States and Great Britain, American Journal of Sociology. Vol.81, p. 579 quoted by S. M. Dahiwale in Emerging Entrepreneurship Among Scheduled Castes.
90. UNESCO Research Centre, (2011), Social Aspects of Small Industries In India, Studied In Hawarth and Bombay, UNESCO Research Centre on Social and Economic Development In Southern Asia, New Delhi.
91. Webber Max, (1958), Effects on Castes and Sub-castes on Entrepreneurship, Talcott Pearsons, Charles Scribner's Sons, New York, pp. 17 To 52.
92. Z. Mars., (1975), Assistance to Small Scale Industries in Kerala, an Indian Case, in Development of Changes, Vol. XVI, No. 2, pp. 14 to 18.

Index